P9-CKT-088

Funny Farm

First published in the United States by St. Martin's Press,
an imprint of St. Martin's Publishing Group

The names of some persons described in this book have been changed.

FUNNY FARM. Copyright © 2021 by Laurie Zaleski. All rights reserved.
Printed in the United States of America. For information, address
St. Martin's Publishing Group, 120 Broadway, New York, NY 10271.

www.stmartins.com

Designed by Steven Seighman

The Library of Congress Cataloging-in-Publication Data is available
upon request.

ISBN 978-1-250-27283-6 (hardcover)
ISBN 978-1-250-27284-3 (ebook)

Our books may be purchased in bulk for promotional, educational,
or business use. Please contact your local bookseller or the Macmillan
Corporate and Premium Sales Department at 1-800-221-7945, extension 5442,
or by email at MacmillanSpecialMarkets@macmillan.com.

First Edition: 2021

10 9 8 7 6 5 4 3 2 1

33614082803510

Funny Farm

MY UNEXPECTED LIFE
WITH 600 RESCUE ANIMALS

Laurie Zaleski

ST. MARTIN'S
PRESS
NEW YORK

For my mom

Contents

Part III: Oh Give Me a Home

Funny Farm

Prologue

It was twilight, that golden hour between daylight and dark, and things were quiet on the farm. All the animals had been fed and returned to their stalls or pens. The chores were done—or as done as they ever can be on a farm, where the work is truly neverending.

In the final ritual of the day, I pulled back the pasture gate, and the horses—I had fifteen at the time—galloped from the fields back into the barn, their manes and tails flying like flags. The sight never failed to thrill me.

The volunteer crew was on its way out, all the fiercely, fanatically, unreasonably dedicated people who've helped keep the Funny Farm and its animals going for the past twenty-odd years.

As for me, I looked forward to a rare quiet evening—if the word "quiet" can ever apply when you live with hundreds of ducks and geese, dogs and cats, pigs and goats, alpacas and horses. The noisiest of all are the peacocks—so regal and beautiful, but with piercing cries that could wake the dead.

But eventually, all the clucking and grunting, neighing and feather-ruffling does settle down, and even the peacocks nod off, usually perched high atop the barn roof, like weathervanes.

Twilight is my favorite time on the farm.

Just in from my day job, I dropped my briefcase, shucked off my dress suit, kicked out of my high heels. and pulled on my farm-girl uniform: Carhartt overalls and shit-kicker boots. I was just about to nuke what remained of yesterday's pizza when I heard the sound of a car crunching onto the gravel driveway. The last person out must have left the gate ajar.

Damn.

I run a graphic design firm, as a contractor, for the federal government. It had been a busy workday—a typical day—with back-to-back meetings and deadlines and lots of fires to extinguish. I was bushed. I wasn't expecting company or, frankly, in the mood for it.

Poking my head out the screen door, I saw a Toyota Camry pull up next to the farmhouse. A twentysomething kid in a rumpled T-shirt and board shorts clambered out of the driver's seat. Then he opened the back door of his car and lifted out an underfed fawn, its long knobby legs feebly kicking.

In a flash, I was out the door.

"Hey!" I shouted. "Do *not* try to dump that animal here."

I was mad, and justifiably so. This happened all too often, people coming to the farm and dropping off unwanted dogs, cats, rabbits, and all kinds of animals, often because the animals are sick, or injured, or old, or in need of some kind of special care.

Usually, the dumpers sneak up under cover of darkness and just toss out the poor creatures, in all kinds of weather, then zoom off. It was the main reason I had installed extra lights, motion detectors, and cameras. But this kid was brazen. He'd driven right in.

Yes, I operate an animal rescue, and most of the animals that live with me—at last count, more than 600—come from less-than-loving circumstances, to say the least. They have been unwanted, abandoned, and sometimes abused. But dumping any animal, for any reason, is irresponsible, cowardly, and cruel. And in most states, including my home state of New Jersey, it's also illegal.

Besides, I mostly rescue farm animals, along with some domestics and a handful of exotics. As a general rule, I don't take deer or other wild animals unless it's short-term, until I can hand them off to a wildlife rehabilitator.

Furious, I charged down the porch steps and brandished my cell phone in the kid's face. "Do you know that dumping animals is illegal? I am taking your license plate number right now, and I've got the cops on speed dial."

To my amazement, as I rattled off this little speech—I had it memorized—he turned to lift a second fawn out of the car.

"You are *not* hearing me," I began.

"Please!" He swung around, a harried look on his face. "*Please.* I've been driving around for five hours, looking for help. I stopped at six different farms. They all said the same thing: 'Go to the Funny Farm.'"

By now, the farm dogs had assembled, prancing and yelping at my heels and edging closer to the nervous fawns. That's when I realized that these were not white-tailed deer at all, but calves: spindly-legged, nearly newborn Jersey calves with caramel-colored coats, big chocolate-brown eyes, and fluttering Bambi lashes. They were unsteady on their feet, ears drooping. The umbilical cords still dangled from their undersides. From the back seat of the Camry wafted the unmistakable smell of manure.

"I can't keep them," said the kid. "My landlord won't let me have—well, cows . . ."

"Where did they come from?"

He averted his eyes. "Auction."

"Oh yeah?" I stared hard at him, hands on my hips.

Then I slid the phone into my pocket. With a shrug and sigh, I braced myself for the latest hard-luck story.

"Okay. Let's hear it."

He perched on the steps of the farmhouse porch, a little calmer, clearly exhausted. He absently scratched behind the ears of my German shepherd, Chucky, who dashed away, came back with a Frisbee, and tried to push it into his palm.

"Chucky, please," I murmured, "not now."

The kid described himself as an activist, committed to saving farm animals from slaughter. At a cattle auction, he had discovered this pair of tiny calves in a metal livestock trailer, practically dead from the heat.

"Not a drop of water," he said, in a voice thick with emotion. "Not a fistful of hay. Jesus, they were on their way to the slaughterhouse. Why couldn't people treat them better on the way?"

"Did you buy them?" I asked.

He stared down at his hands, which dangled between widespread knees. Then he looked at me defiantly. "I *liberated* them."

I understood the compassion that had driven him; I also knew, from long experience, that when you get into animal rescue, you have to at least try to rein in your feelings. If you don't, you'll go crazy, burn out fast, and be way less effective at your mission to save lives and alleviate suffering. This job isn't pretty. It's sure not for the faint of heart.

As for cattle rustling? Well, that's never a great idea.

I also knew that when it comes to cattle, young males—weaners, like these two babies—are less valuable on the open market than females, which also can be used as dairy cows and be bred. Males are more—well, disposable. Often little ones like these were sold for their meat, skin, and "by-products."

I flashed back on Harry Hamburger, the lovable steer I had raised as a farm kid, and the day he just disappeared. Almost thirty years later, I could remember the ache I felt when I realized that Harry was never coming back, except as meat loaf or sloppy joes. After that, I declared I would rather eat mayonnaise sandwiches—and often did—before I would consume meat again. I'd kept that promise.

The sun had almost disappeared, and the sky was a streaky purplish-pink. The calves tottered on their long legs, steadier now and a little less timid. They nipped tentatively at blades of grass. They could not have weighed forty pounds between them, with bony haunches and sticking-out ribs. They looked pitiful.

Pizza would have to wait.

My dogs—Snoop and Freddie, Farley and Chuck—continued to circle the calves, sniffing curiously. I stamped my foot so they would keep their distance. The dogs weren't predatory—they knew better than that—just interested to see who might be joining the family.

At times like these, I couldn't help but think of my mother and the original Funny Farm, the wild and woolly place where I'd grown up. After fleeing a nightmarish marriage, with next to no money, living with three kids in a rundown, one-bedroom house in the woods, Mom had taken a succession of lowly jobs, including one cleaning cages at the local animal shelter. That's when she started bringing home the desperate cases, the animals next in line to be euthanized, until dozens of them roved the woods and fields around our house or lived outside in lean-tos or sheds we built ourselves. Some—including geese, pigs, goats, and an injured, recovering foal—even lived inside with us.

That's when Mom jokingly dubbed our place the Funny Farm—"because it's full of animals, and it's fit for lunatics."

Even at her poorest—and believe me, as Mom would say, most

of the time all she had in her pocket was lint—she couldn't bear to see an animal put to sleep if she could help it. Sometimes, she was scarcely able to keep food on the table. Even so, her rule was: One dollar for the family, one dollar for the animals.

It was Mom who had landed me in this pickle.

Over the kid's shoulder, I looked at the old buckboard wagon near the gate, decorated with strings of twinkling lights. It once was hers, and now was my tribute, a constant reminder of where I had come from and who had raised me.

Well, here we go again, I thought, as I looked at the starving calves. I realized that if I kept them, these sad, sweet babies would grow to be hungry, expensive 1,500-pound bulls or steers, and cost a small fortune to keep up.

Mom, what do you think I should do?

To the kid, I said, "I have T-Bone over there—" I gestured to the big pasture, where a 2,500-pound red Angus steer quietly grazed—"but I guess it isn't a farm without a herd. I think we can make room for a couple more."

His eyes widened, then he dropped his head in his hands, relieved to the point of tears. "Thanks," he said hoarsely. "Thanks."

"First things first," I said. "They'll have to be bottle-fed for a while, and they won't last long if we don't get started right now."

I stood up and brushed the dust from my overalls. "Well? Are you going to help me out, or what?"

PART I

Necessity Is a Mother

Runaways

My mother was twenty-six years old when she grabbed her kids, gathered her courage, and ran for her life. Without a car or even a driver's license, she threw Cathy, Stephen, and me into a borrowed station wagon and burned rubber.

Mom had two speeds: sixty-five and stop. After backing out of our driveway, she lurched over a low curb, made a hard right at the stop sign, then zoomed through our neighborhood, death-gripping the wheel, trying to get out before anyone could spot her.

This was before all cars had seat belts, and with every swerve Cathy, Stephen, and I slid back and forth on the vinyl back seat, piling up against each other but improbably laughing, in spite of our anxiety.

"Heads down back there!" Mom hissed.

When we got out to the highway, she floored it.

We had left home a couple of times before, but after a few days our father would always track us down again and say the magic words that would change Mom's mind and bring her back; once again, we'd turn tail and return to the pretty house on 8 Timber Heights Court.

This time felt different. After hiding out in a motel for a couple of weeks, Mom had brought us back during the afternoon while Dad was still at work, to grab some clothes and towels and toothpaste, just in case he decided to change the locks. This was a first.

It was early December and briskly cold. Already a plastic Santa and sleigh skittered across the roof of our house and a faux-pine wreath graced the front door. A plastic snowman complete with plastic mittens, top hat, and carrot nose had fallen over on the brownish front lawn.

Noiselessly, we slipped inside the house. In the living room, the tinfoil Christmas tree was already up and glistening with a few unwrapped presents stashed underneath: Tonka trucks, Matchbox cars, and Lincoln Logs, books and puzzles, board games like Operation, Twister, Parcheesi, and Chinese checkers. I saw my own little pile, which included coloring books and crayons and all things Barbie: the pink convertible sports car that went with Barbie's Dream House, Barbie's Country Camper, and Barbie's palomino, Dancer—or was it Dallas?

My mother dashed from room to room, throwing utensils and clothing and toiletries into a pillowcase. I made a dive for the Barbie stuff, but she shook her head firmly. "Only what you *need*."

"Mom . . ."

"Okay then! One or two toys. But hurry it up."

I wanted to take my Barbie styling head—a disembodied, life-size plastic head with its own makeup products and flaxen hair you could set, tease, and brush. But before I could lug it out of my room, she said, "*Leave the head.* Now get a move on!"

In less than forty minutes, the four of us were back in the car and back on the road. As we drove out of the cul-de-sac, I couldn't help but look back at the big brick house with the sloping lawn surrounded by towering old oak trees, now stripped of their leaves.

On the roof, our plastic Santa raised his hand and rocked gently in the wind. It looked as if he were waving goodbye.

This time, I knew we wouldn't be coming back.

In the mid-1970s, the four-lane Black Horse Pike was the main route between Philadelphia and the Jersey Shore, surrounded by farms and farmers' markets, custard stands and roadhouse taverns.

There were a few billboards—for Zaberer's restaurant ("home of the Zaberized cocktail!") and Coppertone suntan lotion ("Don't be a paleface!"), featuring a cherubic little golden-haired girl who looked over her shoulder as her swimsuit was tugged down by a small dog.

From Memorial Day to Labor Day, at least on weekends, the pike was bumper to bumper with summer people—called "shoobies" by the locals, because they supposedly used to travel to the beach with their lunch in shoeboxes.

But in the off-season, the pike was nearly deserted, and a good thing, too. As Mom made her getaway, she was free to veer in and out of lanes, unencumbered by other traffic except the occasional tractor or big rig.

When Cathy and I popped up for a look, Mom turned around—still barreling down the road—and jabbed a finger into our faces.

"Did I tell you to keep your heads down?"

Cathy pointed at the highway ahead, at the weaving front end of the car. "Mom," she cried, saucer-eyed. "Mom!"

Mom turned back, and, in a gentler voice said, "Please, just keep out of sight, kids. We don't have far to go—just around the corner."

We ducked down again, our heads in our laps like it was an air-raid drill. Then we turned onto Route 42, a parallel road also called the North-South Freeway. A few minutes more, and at last the station wagon slowed and started bumping over an unpaved surface.

Stephen was crouched in the middle. Over his small blond head, Cathy and I glanced at each other apprehensively.

Door to door, our dramatic getaway had taken the better part of an hour, but actually deposited us less than ten minutes from Dad's house on Timber Heights Court, part of a larger development called Timber Heights, in the town of Turnersville, New Jersey. Mom had deliberately taken a circuitous route, looping in and out of side streets and gas station lots and seasonal farmers' markets, keeping one eye on the rearview mirror in case she was being followed. She knew Dad wouldn't willingly relinquish control of his family, whom he considered his rightful possessions, much like his houses, his clothing, and his Cadillacs.

At last the station wagon eased to a stop. Mom exhaled. Rising up again, Cathy, Stephen, and I peered out the windows for the first look at our new home.

It was plopped down in an overgrown field off the main drag, about a quarter mile behind a sort of strip mall. The mall—a slab of asphalt with two tannish multistory buildings and a low-slung, prefab modular home—had a John Hancock insurance office, an accounting and tax service, a health spa, and an RV dealership called the Hitcharama. Most of it, including the house, was owned by the tax man, Al Clark.

I'm not quite sure how my mom first met this Mr. Clark—I think it was a friend-of-a-friend kind of deal—but he must have taken pity on her, a valiant young mother on the run from her brutal husband. He only asked for a hundred dollars a month in rent. That was peanuts, even in the 1970s.

There was only one problem: the house was a shell, not fit to live in. It could not have been legally habitable.

Yet this, Mom had promised, would be our "brand-new start."

Climbing out of the car, Cathy and I took one look at the dingy, one-story structure and started to wail like banshees.

"Is this the place we're going to live? We can't live here. It's *ugly*."

Believe me, in this case ugly would have been a compliment. The house—really, it was no more than half a house—was built of cinder blocks partially covered with fake tan brickwork. Square and squat with a pitched roof, it was almost hidden at the edge of the pine woods, in a dusty clearing surrounded by waist-high weeds.

Its few windows were broken or cracked, and one of the wooden sills hung down, as if someone had stepped on it to crawl inside. If there once had been steps out front, they were long gone—it was a straight drop, five feet from the doorsill to the ground. The next lot over was a dump, an Everest of old tires, aluminum siding, broken bricks, construction waste, and other trash, plus a couple of abandoned crap cars with their rusted hoods up and gaping.

We would soon discover that this place, never occupied, had turned into a hangout for local teenagers who came here to smoke, drink, shoot at rats and squirrels, and otherwise run wild. In other words, it was a squatters' shack. Galaxies away from the pretty red brick house in Timber Heights.

So I think Mr. Clark's decision to rent to us, while compassionate, was also self-serving. If we lived there, those gangs of roving hooligans would stop breaking in.

At least that was the working theory, which soon would be disproven.

We must have made a pitiful sight, lugging our sad little bags—literally, brown paper Acme bags, plus a few flowered pillowcases and one suitcase, stuffed with the things we'd been able to grab while our father was at his job. Mom was smiling, but in a strange, fixed way that wasn't even half-happy.

I clutched my favorite baby doll, Penny—Mom's doll when she was a kid—and let my tears fall onto her molded rubber head. Penny made a "waa, waa" sound when you pressed on her neck, and on that day we cried together.

All of us kids were upset, and wired, too—from stress, lack of sleep, and a steady diet of junk food. We had been living out of a suitcase, four people shoehorned into a single motel room, sleeping on two narrow beds with thin mattresses and springs that dug into our backs at night.

Before that, we had witnessed some pretty harrowing episodes at home. Seeing Dad slap Mom around had left us freaked out and agitated, clingy and nervous. We kids had caught some of his rage, too—he'd once backhanded Cathy when she wouldn't eat her mashed potatoes and tried to physically force me, with his hands around the base of my throat, to swallow a hunk of rubbery steak. Once an argument spilled from the house into the garage. There he swung at Mom with a two-by-four plank, but struck three-year-old Stephen instead, making blood gush from his ear.

As long as we children stayed in line and out of the way, we usually weren't Dad's targets. But if any of us dared to disobey or even show by expression or gesture that we weren't wholly compliant and happy, he could flip, just like that, from mild-mannered suburban squire to that "other," a brute who didn't care if he hurt us, and sometimes even seemed to enjoy it.

It was like a ritual. He would make a great show of unbuckling his wide leather belt, slowly draw it out of the belt loops, carefully wind the belt around his fist, then swat at our legs and behinds until we were running in circles around the room, trying to stay clear of the stinging blows. In such moments, his face would seem almost unrecognizable—like a Halloween mask, twisted and grotesque, almost purple with rage. And if we cried, so much the worse for us.

"Crying, are you, crybaby? I'll give you something to cry about."

I remember tipping my head back, desperately trying to keep the tears from spilling over.

Mom would send us to our rooms to wait out the storm, and he would turn her into a tackling dummy. Huddling in my room, I cringed to hear the flesh-on-flesh sound that meant he was striking her.

Curiously, though, on rare occasions Mom was able to talk him down, stop him in his tracks, almost as if she were waking him from a bad dream. At those times, he would shake his head, drop the belt, and shrug it off.

I don't know if he felt remorseful, because he never apologized, but the incident would blessedly be over for that moment. Until the next time.

For all the upheaval in our lives, there was a strange, indefinable excitement about hiding out, moving from motel to motel, keeping one step ahead of our pursuer. For little kids, it seemed like an adventure to stay in a strange place, to load up buckets of ice from the ice machine and play around the pool, even though it was covered by a canvas. In a bizarre way, it was almost fun.

Our hideaways were bedbuggy dives or no-tell motels where businessmen from Philadelphia or Cherry Hill traveled for their trysts. I'm not talking the Marriott, which would have been five-star opulence to people like us.

We lived on Cheetos and peanut butter crackers and Sprite from the inevitable lobby vending machine, with Chuckles candy for dessert—a diet of pure sugar, fat, and chemical additives. Occasionally, Mom would shop at a local market for normal food, like bread, cheese and milk, and we'd stick the groceries on the frozen windowsill at night to keep them cold. Sometimes if we begged, she would treat us to takeout pizza. Then we'd all pile up on those beds and fall into a collective carbohydrate coma.

Our real pacifier was the TV—usually a big, boxy set bolted high onto the motel room wall. Like little zombies, we would gape up at it for hours on end, watching cartoons in the morning, quiz shows and soap operas in the afternoon and, at night, sitcoms. *The Brady Bunch. The Partridge Family. Happy Days.* All about wacky but loving families who stuck together no matter what, and solved their problems in thirty minutes, minus commercials.

Our vagabond life, though fun while it lasted, ended in that little house in the woods.

Lugging our paper bags and pillowcases, we trudged around to the back door, grumbling all the way. Stepping gingerly across the threshold, we found that the ugly house was even uglier on the inside, and bone-chillingly cold.

The dull plasterboard walls were pocked with holes, like someone had taken a sledgehammer and just started swinging. The floorboards were creaky, spongy in places from sitting water, and strewn with trash: beer bottles, cigarette butts, and powder-coated sandwich bags that Mom quickly kicked under a pile of newspapers.

The kitchen was an afterthought—appliance hookups, but no appliances, not even a refrigerator. And the bathroom! It was a blue nightmare—blue bathtub, blue toilet, blue tiled walls with blackened grout, and a blue tub with an unspeakably grimy ring. Though the house had never been officially occupied, the bathroom definitely had been used. Mold crawled along the baseboards, spiders hung in every corner, and there was an awful, sour smell that made my stomach turn cartwheels.

Cathy, usually the stoic, erupted in noisy tears. "I wanna go home!"

Mom sagged, as if she'd just realized she was carrying the world's weight. Then, summoning some inner grit—some inner *something*— she stood up tall again and pasted on her determined smile.

"C'mon now, kids! A little elbow grease, a little Lysol, and in no time, this place will be nice and cozy. Did you take a look out back? Those are fruit trees. We'll make pie! There are acres of woods."

She opened a door that led into a small square room. "The bedroom. Laurie and Cathy, once we get a bed, you two can share, and Stephen and I will bunk out here for a while." She looked encouragingly at us girls. "Just think. Like a slumber party every night!"

At this I perked up, but Cathy's tears turned to angry sobs. At home, she had the prettiest room: ballet-slipper pink with sage-green walls, a canopy bed, and gauzy bedding edged in eyelet lace. I didn't dare to go in there without saying Mother-may-I. Now she was being asked to share a room with her messy little sister, and she didn't like it.

"No fair," she bawled, like I had cooties or something. "Why do I have to be in with *Laurie*?"

At first, I was stung. Then I got mad. If Cathy didn't want to share with me, then I didn't want to share with her. "No fair!" I said. "I don't want to be in with *Cathy*!"

That was Stephen's cue. Standing in the center of the room, he set to baying, like a little hound dog puppy. "I wanna go home. I wanna see my dad."

That was it. Mom blew. She threw down the suitcase and kicked an empty tin can so hard it went rocketing into the wall. "Okay!"

she shouted. "Go ahead and cry, all of you! Cry me a goddamned river! The more you cry, the less you'll pee!"

With that outburst, Stephen's mouth snapped shut, and Cathy stopped crying. I just gaped, stunned to hear my ladylike mother talk like that. But through my tears, it occurred to me that this sounded funny.

The more you cry, the less you'll pee.

On a dime, I went from crying to snickering, and so did Mom and the other kids. Somehow, that moment saved the day for all of us.

She swiped a quick hand across her eyes, then scooped up Stephen and patted him until his sobs turned to hiccups. Over his shoulder she looked down at Cathy and me.

"Look girls, I'm sorry, but this is where we live now—" Again we started to squawk, but she threw up a palm. "Not a word! I need you to deal with this and help your brother deal with it, too. Come on, let's start bringing that stuff in from the car."

She gazed wearily around the place, shaking her head with a "who-am-I-kidding" look.

"We'll make this place a home," she said. "Nice and cozy."

By dinnertime, we had cleared out a lot of the junk. First Mom went through it all, I guess to pick out any broken glass or recreational items, like condoms or rolling papers. Then she helped us shovel fistfuls into garbage bags, with high fives all around when we'd made a good dent. We swept what was left into a pile in the corner of the living room.

Inevitably, one by one, all of us had to go to the bathroom, and Mom announced that we'd have to go outside, in the woods. She held up a roll of toilet paper.

"Like camping!" she said brightly.

Stephen didn't seem to mind, but Cathy and I were horrified and refused until we were squirming so much, we could refuse no more. Out there in the frigid December, squatting behind scrubby pines, we bared our bottoms like the Coppertone girl, relieved ourselves quickly, then yanked up our pants and raced each other back to the house.

It dawned on us that not only did the bathroom not work—because no running water—but the heat and lights didn't work, either—because no electricity. We were shivering and our breath made frosty clouds in the air. Mom pulled some blankets in from the car, dragged them into the middle of the living room—because no furniture—and we sat cross-legged in a circle.

"Like camping!" said Mom.

I looked at Cathy glumly. If this was camping, it was camping with all the discomfort and none of the s'mores. But dusk soon gave way to darkness. It had been a tumultuous day and we surrendered to exhaustion. It couldn't have been seven o'clock when everyone collapsed in a huddle, curling up against each other to keep warm, and fell dead asleep.

Hours later I woke up, in darkness so impenetrable I couldn't see my own hands. It took me a moment to remember I wasn't in my own bed or in a bed in a motel room, but on the floor of this ugly half-house in the woods. Rolling over, I barely made out the silhouettes of my brother and sister, buried under blankets, their breathing even and deep.

Then I saw my mom, illuminated in a square of moonlight slanting through a bare window. Sitting upright in the blanket pile, she rocked back and forth, back and forth, with her head in her hands.

"Mommy . . ."

At the sound of my voice, her shoulders tensed. In a low, fierce voice, she whispered, "It's all right, Laurie. Go back to sleep."

Instead I scooted across the floor, trying not to lose my covers or my doll, and curved my body around hers. "What's the matter, Mommy?" I said. Like I didn't know what was the matter.

In the thin greenish moonlight, I could see her uplifted face in profile. She grimaced, and I couldn't tell if she was laughing or crying.

"Oh, Laurie," she said. "I just hate camping."

Animal Tails

Yogi and Cooper

I named the newborn Jersey calves Yogi and Boo-Boo. With good food and care, they grew from skinny bags of bones into big strapping boys, about 1,200 pounds each. A veterinarian friend who is also a farmer adopted Boo-Boo. Yogi continues to live at the Funny Farm.

As a yearling, Yogi had the run of the place, and was happiest on visiting days, lolling on the ground as children crawled all over him. That changed when he accidentally hooked a child's denim suspender on one of his budding horns, lifting the boy bodily off the ground.

No one was hurt; in fact, the boy's mom pulled out her phone to snap a picture of her son, both laughing as he dangled in mid-air. But for obvious reasons, I couldn't risk letting that happen again. A cow's horns aren't decorative but defensive, and potentially dangerous.

I decided not to remove Yogi's horns when he was a calf, which is called "disbudding," because I felt the process was cruel. And though I knew cows' horns can be removed later in life for safety reasons, this is major surgery, and very painful, because the horns contain blood vessels and nerve endings as well as cartilage and bone. I didn't want to put my big boy through an ordeal like that. So I decided that on visiting days, I would keep Yogi in a broad, fenced-in pasture. That way, he could see and enjoy our guests, but at a safe remove.

Alas, even behind the fence, those sharp horns were almost the undoing of an alpaca named Cooper. Cooper had been surrendered to the Funny Farm along with his sibling, Quinny, because they shared a minor genetic imperfection: a kink in their tails that, for some reason, made them unacceptable to breeders. Quinny was frail from the start and when he died, Yogi and Cooper became best buds.

In a full coat of cold-weather fleece, Cooper looks almost as big as Yogi. But when he's shorn for the summer, you can see how slender he is, and the two of them together look like Laurel and Hardy. One summer day, shortly after Cooper was shorn, he and Yogi were at the pasture fence, accepting treats from our visitors, when they tussled over a carrot. Yogi swung his big head in the direction of Cooper, who had no fibrous coat to absorb the impact. That's when one of Yogi's sharp horns struck Coop in the belly, accidentally goring him.

A volunteer saw it happen and sent out the SOS. Another volunteer, who is also an emergency medical technician, sprinted at top speed to the pasture, quickly joined by a third volunteer with EMT training. By the time I got there, Cooper was standing quietly, a gash opening up his side. His intestines were actually spilling out on the ground, yet he never made a sound. He was such a good patient.

The injury was bad. The EMT calmly assessed the injury, asked for a bucket of clean water, and rinsed the innards before gently nudging them back into place. Then he bound Cooper's belly with medical tape and a sterile pad to hold the intestines in. Volunteers surrounded Cooper and held his head to comfort him.

Meanwhile, I phoned the New Bolton Center, the veterinary hospital of the University of Pennsylvania, about ninety minutes to the north (as you can imagine, I have them on speed dial, too!). With help from a few other volunteers, we loaded Cooper into the large back seat of the Funny Farm truck and took off. The ninety-minute drive took just sixty-five minutes, but it seemed like nine hours. When we arrived at the hospital, a team of doctors was waiting to rush him into surgery.

I don't know if Yogi realized that his playful poke had harmed Cooper, but he was inconsolable without his friend. That first night, I could hear him bawling like a baby. For the next week, he lay dejectedly on the ground, head slumped down, and refused to respond when we called his name. He rejected all his favorite treats, including carrots. He missed his buddy.

Luckily, Yogi had also missed all the alpaca's vital organs. Cooper survived and returned with great fanfare a week later, almost as good as new, with his stitches healing nicely. The first thing he did was trot up to the pasture fence to see Yogi, as if to say, "Hey, pal, no hard feelings." Yogi perked up right away.

Obviously, though, we couldn't reunite the best friends until we fitted Yogi with some kind of protective gear to keep him from hurting Coop, or another animal or person. First, we tried sticking tennis balls on the ends of his horns, which made him look like he had just beamed down from outer space. Yogi easily scraped them off. Then we stuck on foam swimming noodles, with no better luck.

After that, a friend of the farm sent us a pair of clear silicone horn guards, with bulbous, rounded ends that, alas, looked like a pair of adult toys. Every time the volunteers looked at Yogi in those silvery guards, they burst out laughing. Poor Yogi was mortified, especially when he knew 50,000 people were watching on Facebook Live, and though we stuck the guards on good and proper, and even secured them with hot-pink duct tape, eventually Yogi shucked them off as well.

We're still working on a solution. Until then, or until Cooper's winter coat grows back in, the animals will have to keep a fence between them. This is just one of the many odd, but enduring friendships at the Funny Farm.

2

We Were the Joneses

My parents hailed from Port Richmond, a working-class, largely Polish American section of Philadelphia that looks out on the Delaware River. The neighborhood, known as "Little Poland," was gritty, blue-collar, clannish, and proud. The people were rough around the edges but hardworking and kind.

Back then, Philadelphia was called "the workshop of the world," and good-paying work was plentiful. Port Richmonders labored at the navy shipyard or the Jack Frost sugar refinery or the city's carpet mills and textile factories. People who got jobs at Gulf Oil or the Atlantic Richfield refinery in South Philly kept those jobs for decades, for lifetimes, and got their kids in, too.

After work, the grown-ups would sit on their front stoops, drinking Ortlieb's or Ballantine beer and eating kielbasa from Czerw's as the kids played up and down the sidewalk: half-ball and pimple-ball, hopscotch and buck-buck, Red Rover and Miss Mary Mack.

To this day, it's not uncommon for generations of Port Richmond families to live on the same street in the same type of narrow three-story row house they used to call a "trinity," also known as a "Father, Son, and Holy Ghost."

This is where Mom and Dad grew up, the place that shaped their values and choices through its culture, traditions, and, perhaps most of all, its faith. Among the *Polonia amerykańska*, or people of Polish ancestry, there were also people of Irish, Italian, and German descent, each tending to cluster on their own streets. It was sort of an ethnic melting pot with one thing in common: everybody was Catholic.

I've always likened my mom's name to Irish poetry (or maybe an Irish drinking song): Annie McNulty. She had fair skin, lots of golden-brown curls, and a cascade of freckles. She attended an all-girls Catholic high school called Little Flower, named for Saint Therese of Lisieux. She briefly thought of joining the order of sisters who taught there, the Carmelites.

Among Catholic families, it was still considered a privilege to give at least one child to the convent or priesthood. Mom's parents—my Grandma Ida McNulty, who ran a candy store, and Pop-Pop Ed, a city councilman known to his constituents as "Happy" or "Hap"—would have been proud to see Annie take the veil. It still amazes me to see a photo of her as a teenager, dressed in a cream-colored novice's habit, her hands clasped prayerfully before her, looking like the Virgin Mary about to shoot up into heaven.

"I almost became a nun," Mom would joke years later. "Then I met the devil."

That handsome devil down the block, Richie Zaleski.

It's an old story, maybe the oldest of all old stories. Anne McNulty and Richard Zaleski fell in love like tripping into an open manhole: one wrong move followed by a long dark plunge.

Giddily, and in the flush of new passion, they planned a future and didn't bother about getting to know each other. Just like that, Mom ditched the nunnery and hitched her wagon to Dad's star.

And he was a skyrocket, to be sure. Richard Zaleski was supersmart at math and had a nose for business. He went from Northeast Catholic High School (all boys) to LaSalle College, and then on to Xavier University in Cincinnati, where he earned an MBA and an MA in economics along with his teaching credentials.

Mom was always a letter-writer, and when her beau was in Ohio, she became his faithful correspondent. In a letter that survives from 1965, she wrote, "My darling Richie, I am so anxious to see you that the days go by like weeks. . . . I shall always love you a little more than yesterday and a little less than tomorrow. With all my love forever and ever, your future wife, Anne (Mrs. Richard Zaleski xxx ooo)."

On the back of the envelope, she added, in her beautiful Catholic-school cursive, "SWAK" (sealed with a kiss) and "*Przyrzekam, że zawsze będę was kochać.*" ("I promise I will love you always" in Polish).

They were just eighteen and twenty when they promised to love, honor, and, in my mother's case, obey, all the years of their lives. I think of them as the perfect fifties-era couple—except by then it was the 1960s. All the old social mores were being kicked over, rebellion was in the air, the sexual revolution and free love were in vogue, and nontraditional weddings had already become the style.

But Annie and Richie did things the Port Richmond way: according to God's holy ordinance. In wedding photos, they look just like the bride and groom atop the cake, and Mom's bell-shaped white satin gown nicely concealed her pregnancy.

A few months later, along came Cathy. I followed like clockwork the next year. They kept trying until they produced a boy, Stephen, who arrived eighteen months after me. Only then, as far as Mom and Dad were concerned, was the Kodachrome picture complete. They moved from Philly to Turnersville, New Jersey, in the southern part of the state because it had great schools and, as everyone knew, the suburbs were better for the kids. In early photos of the family, we look like a postcard of happy domesticity: Greetings from Pleasant Valley.

And for a time, it really was true. We were the lucky ones. The happy ones. The Zaleskis, of Timber Heights Court, in the prettiest house on the nicest block in one of the most desirable parts of Turnersville.

The Zaleskis didn't have to keep up with the Joneses. We *were* the Joneses.

Everybody in town seemed to know us, and they especially knew Dad, who by then was an up-and-coming economics professor at Camden County College and had made a pile of money in the stock market. Before he turned thirty, we already had three houses: a vacation house in the Pocono Mountains, a massive summer place at the Jersey Shore, and the house in Turnersville. Dad played the stock market like he played cards. And he usually came up aces.

As for Mom, she was the happy homemaker, demure but fashionable in her minidresses and capris with beautifully coiffed hair and flawless makeup. She was the type who wouldn't be caught dead in a T-shirt or sweats or with curlers in her hair. She was up at dawn, and before the rest of us, so that by breakfast she looked like she'd just stepped out of a Breck shampoo ad. It was important to her to please my dad and be what he wanted in a wife: a helpmate, homemaker, and armpiece; smiling and submissive, like a mannequin.

He certainly was what she wanted, what every woman supposedly wanted in those days: a good provider, smart and successful, and respected in the community. Dad was president of the school board and coach of the softball team. He was on all the different committees. When he walked down the street people made way, and he would wave like he was in a parade. Mr. Wonderful. It made me proud to walk alongside him.

He was less popular on our circle. Mr. Wonderful was also the neighborhood grouch, who crabbed at kids for playing near his driveway and would raise a stink about a barking dog or a pickup ball game. Dad never backed down from a confrontation and never, ever doubted that he was right. Our neighbors gave him a wide berth, but they still respected and deferred to him. Because he was a man of means.

All his life Dad drove only Cadillacs, and spent hours on Saturdays washing, waxing, and Simonizing, then rubbing down the leather interior with Armor All. Every year or so, he would trade in his current Caddy for a newer, longer model, always with the shark-like tailfins, always in a show-off color: Daytona Yellow, Cambridge Red, Byzantine Gold.

He looked good behind the wheel, dashing, with the bluest eyes—they were periwinkle blue, the same shade as the crayon. He was fair-haired and lightened his hair even more with lemon juice and Sun-In, a spray-on product that promised "end of the summer highlights before the end of the week." He tried to get his hair to do that Kennedy swoop in the front, but all the Brylcreem in the world couldn't do the trick.

Dad had closets full of clothes, maybe even more than Mom, in all the latest mod styles. He exercised in our backyard and didn't mind at all if people noticed him out there, bare-chested and tan, lifting weights and doing push-ups or riding shirtless on his power lawnmower.

Dad's only flaw, as he saw it, was his profile—he had a prominent nose that bothered him, and years later he would have it fixed, along with his eyelids. But those imperfections couldn't have troubled him too much, because he was always a charmer.

Especially around the ladies.

My father always had a thing for blondes. Jayne Mansfield. Joey Heatherton. Tuesday Weld. All the beautiful bombshells of the fifties and sixties. So when he started dating Annie McNulty, a natural brunette, she went platinum, a sugary, almost white-blonde color, and stayed that way as long as she was married.

In her bathroom at home, next to the vanity, was a whole shelf full of wigs and falls and clip-on French and Grecian curls from the Eva Gabor and Frederick's of Hollywood lines. Some were made of real hair and some were "carefree Dynel," the same stuff they use to patch boat decks.

I was fascinated but a little disturbed to see these hairpieces perched on a line of blank-faced Styrofoam heads. Their empty faces rattled me and I wanted to draw on features, so all the wig-heads would be smiling, like my Barbie head.

By the early seventies, with the women's movement picking up steam, more of Mom's friends and contemporaries were heading into the workplace, mostly as teachers and nurses, secretaries and librarians. Annie, on the other hand, like the "dear little old-fashioned girl" in the song, was content to stay at home, where her husband wanted her.

But even she must have chafed at the restrictions that were imposed on her. Dad wouldn't allow her to drive, so she had to run all her errands on a bicycle, with little Stephen perched in a basket on top of the handlebars, and Cathy and I on a two-seat carrier bolted to the rear wheelbase. He wouldn't let her have a credit card, so she paid for the groceries out of a cash allowance, which he handed over every Saturday in a bank envelope.

I cannot imagine being happy in such a dictatorship, but Mom must have interpreted these rules as proof of her husband's love and devotion. To her way of thinking, he was the man of the house, the breadwinner whose only thought was to keep her comfortable, happy, and protected—like Jack Spratt's wife, safe in her own private pumpkin shell.

And, heck, even in the seventies, this wasn't an unusual way of thinking. It wasn't until 1974 that American women got the right to hold a credit card in their own names.

At home, a housekeeper did most of the cooking and cleaning. Our nanny, a patient, warmhearted Black woman named Nettie, tended to us kids. A landscaper came each week to keep our lawn Miracle-Gro green, like a golf course or the Astroturf at Connie Mack Stadium.

Mom didn't have a whole lot to do, not to say she didn't keep busy. She volunteered for bake sales and white elephant sales. She raised money for Jerry's Kids and the March of Dimes. She received a commendation for working with the "retarded children" of our parish.

And of course, she donated to any charity or group that helped animals. Mom would have had a dozen animals if Dad had permitted it, and one of our favorite Saturday trips was to visit Duffield's Animal Farm in Washington Township, to see and pet the sheep and goats. But Dad only allowed us one pet, a pretty black cat. Our Spooky.

Mom had hobbies, too. She was a gifted ceramicist, and her hand-painted plates and figurines adorned our walls and the sill of our bay window. I remember a painted figurine of a boy and his dog. The figures were beautifully rendered, with colors so lifelike and true I wouldn't have been amazed to see the boy turn his head or the dog wag its tail. Mom was an artist. Given a different life, she might have been a painter or sculptor. But my real childhood treasure was a light-up ceramic snowman with a frosted, crushed-glass finish that glistened like real freshly fallen snow. Mom made one for each of us kids, and every Christmas she would unpack them and put them on our nightstands. I loved to wake up in the middle of the night and see my snowman, all aglow in the darkness.

Mom was good at needlework and made lots of our clothes as well as her own, on a heavy Singer sewing machine with an old-style foot treadle. I remember the showstopper in her wardrobe: a pair of crocheted, teal-colored hot pants and matching halter top that she wore with patent leather heels or white go-go boots, to show off her gorgeous legs, and pantyhose that made her skin feel like an emery board.

Mom didn't go in for jewelry much, but was thrilled when Dad gave her a ranch mink stole. Back then—before she learned how minks are farmed—she could hardly wait for cold weather so she could wear her stole without being called stuck-up.

Best of all, Mom was very musical. I loved it when she played the grand piano in our living room, singing tunes from Broadway shows.

Our folks were so highly regarded that when they gave a party, it was in the society page of the local newspaper: "Professor and Mrs. Richard Zaleski entertained at home on Saturday . . ." Then it would mention all the personages who stopped by.

Mom was the hostess with the mostest. When guests were expected, she would prepare all her specialties—curried crab canapés, ham and macaroni bake, smothered pork chops, and for dessert, a fluorescent orange Jell-O party mold, with grapes and maraschino cherries suspended inside the quivering mass. She contributed all these recipes to the Camden County College Faculty Wives Association cookbook, called *Food for Thought*.

On those party evenings, she would wear her favorite creation, a low-cut red velvet dress with a slit skirt and a neckline edged with seed pearls. It just matched our red shag carpet. On those nights we kids would be hustled off to bed early, but I'd crouch at the top of the stairs, listening to the muffled conversations, the clink of cocktail glasses, and Mom at the piano, playing songs from *Carousel, Camelot, The King and I*, and her favorite, *Annie Get Your Gun*.

In her sweet, husky voice, she would sing a ballad from that show: "They say that falling in love is wonderful . . ."

And I just knew as she sang it that she was looking fondly at my father. It used to give me a warm, safe feeling, like being wrapped up in a protective blanket.

Then, for comic effect, she would follow it up with another song from the same show: "You Can't Get a Man with a Gun."

And the grown-ups would laugh, and the pleasant sound would roll up the steps in waves. There was something magical about those nights. Eventually, I'd crawl off to bed, but I always kept my door open, so I could hear the happy sounds and murmuring talk as I drifted off to sleep. It was my favorite lullaby.

A few times a year, we would go to Olan Mills, the photo studio at the local mall, for family portraits. There, against a faux backdrop of autumn leaves or waving palms or snowy pines, we looked picture-perfect: proud parents and smiling children in our perfectly starched Sunday best, everybody saying "cheese."

In one photo, Cathy and I are hilariously dressed in matching red-and-white gingham jumpers, with saggy-kneed white leggings and patent-leather Mary Janes (and, yes, they really did reflect up).

Those were the wonder years, and that's how I remember my family back then: a picture of contentment.

But nowadays, looking at the same photographs, I find myself searching for the fault lines. Does my mother's smile look a little forced? Does my dad seem a little too jovial? Why isn't Stephen smiling here? And why am I smiling so hard?

Behind closed doors, the happy-family veneer was already starting to fracture.

The whispering had begun about Dad, that he had been seen out with this or that girl—often one of his college students. For the longest time my mom didn't believe the rumors, or refused to.

"Laurie," she insisted, years later, when I was old enough to understand such things, "we were *happy*. I couldn't have been wrong about that. I thought people were just jealous."

Then a letter came in the mail—typewritten, anonymous, from someone who identified herself as the mother of one of the college girls. "Mrs. Zaleski, I am a parent, too, and I feel compelled to tell you that your husband . . ."

Dad denied it vehemently, up, down, and sideways. Mom wanted to believe him—she needed to, she tried to, with heart and soul. But the letter opened her eyes, and suddenly all the clues were there in plain sight, unavoidable, like Dad's weekly committee meetings and after-school functions, which always ran late into the evening and never required her presence.

Mom turned into an investigator, not to catch her husband in the act but in hopes of proving his detractors wrong. One night, she dressed up in a trench coat and a dark wig like Agent 99 in *Get Smart* and trailed Dad to a bar the next town over. There he sat in a leatherette booth nuzzling one of his young girlfriends, a nineteen-ish blonde-on-blonde girl who giggled at his every alleged witticism. Though Mom sat directly across from him, he didn't recognize her.

Even then, caught in the act, Dad tried to convince her it wasn't what it seemed.

"I saw you, Rich," said Mom tearfully. "I saw you."

With the cat out of the bag, Dad ventured to suggest an "open marriage"—swinging, wife-swapping, like in a popular movie of the time, *Bob and Carol and Ted and Alice*. Among the freewheeling couples of that era, and perhaps more among the academic types Dad palled around with, fidelity in marriage had become laughably old-fashioned. Wasn't it far more realistic, Dad argued, and even more loving, to embrace many sexual partners? In his view, it was a good deal all around: men could be men, and now, women could get in on the action, too.

It must have been heartbreaking for Mom, who had never loved another man, who had expected to spend a lifetime loving this one. Free love? The former future nun wasn't buying it.

In the beginning, their battles took place behind closed doors. But soon the arguments got louder and louder until one night, when my mother dared to talk back, Dad landed the first blow.

So twice we left and twice Mom brought us back. Each time we returned, we all would tiptoe around, so afraid of doing something that would ignite the next explosion. This, too, infuriated my father.

"What's the matter with this family?" he would bellow. "Can't I get a smile and hello when I walk in the door?"

The atmosphere was horribly strained. Mom tried to resume her role as the happy homemaker, but by this time it was pure playacting. The tension was so thick even Spooky could feel it. He abandoned his favorite spot in the window to hide under the sofa, peering out with unblinking green eyes.

The end, when it came, was sudden and violent.

It was a dark and stormy night—really, it was—right between Thanksgiving and Christmas. Our tree, one of those silvery aluminum jobs that opened like an umbrella, had been hauled up from the cellar and partially decorated. Christmas cards were displayed around the fireplace and propped up on every table, and our stockings hung from the mantel.

Mom had begun her annual cookie-baking marathon, and the house smelled warmly of gingerbread and shortbread and *kruis-chiki*, Polish fritters also called "angel wings" or "bow ties," made of eggs, cream, and flour and drizzled with confectioner's sugar and honey.

Then she dug into the basement closet and brought out our ceramic snowmen, which she had wrapped in newspaper and packed away the previous year.

I don't know what set it off. By that time, my dad was always spoiling for a fight and Mom had reached a breaking point, too. All I remember is that I was playing in my bedroom when it started, with voices raised downstairs.

I jumped off the bed and stood at the open door of my room, twisting the doorknob behind me and trembling. They started shouting, then screaming, a terrible duet that made the minutes drag on like hours. Mom cried out in fear, then in pain, and I heard the sound of Dad hitting her. I raced to the top of the stairwell and started screaming.

"Please don't! Please don't hurt my mom!" My sister joined in the piercing cries.

Something crashed, and, scared as we were, Cathy and I bounded down the stairs to find Mom sprawled back on the sofa, her legs bloodied, with one of the cherished ceramic snowmen in pieces at her feet. At first, Dad was nowhere in sight. Then, with an ungodly roar he charged up the steps from the basement, wielding a woodman's ax.

More than forty years later, my memory of that moment is as indelible as if it happened yesterday: I see the ax swinging and the glint of its blade and the squint of my father's periwinkle-blue eyes. I see the streaks of blood on my mother's legs. As a result of this fight, for the rest of her life she would have multiple small scars, like tiny broken blood vessels, all over her calves and thighs.

That's when something possessed me—I'm talking *Exorcist*-style possession, minus the spinning head and pea-soup vomit. Any fear I'd felt the instant before vanished. I threw my body on top of my mother's like a shield, and kicked and flailed and shrieked in a guttural voice. Cathy piled on, too. To get to Mom, he would have to go through her defenders, five- and six-year-old girls. He backed off that time and Mom shouted at us to get back upstairs, out of harm's way.

Amazingly, no one on our quiet circle called the cops or tried to intervene, though they must have heard the hell being raised that day.

The fight continued on and off for hours, a cacophony of shouting and crying and busting and smashing. Late in the afternoon, when the house fell still, once again I stood at the door of my bedroom, a little sentinel, listening hard, hoping the hostilities were done with. When I heard nothing more, I began to breathe more easily.

It had only been a ceasefire. The battle started again, worse than before. I dashed into my sister's room just as Mom ran up to the second floor, followed by Dad, who held a carving knife. He barricaded the three of us—Mom, Cathy, me—in Cathy's room, then lay in the doorway on the floor, the knife in his clenched hand. Stephen, by this time fast asleep in his room, thankfully missed it all.

The standoff seemed to last forever. Cathy and I huddled together, squalling, as Mom tried to reason with my father. All the fight was out of her by that time; she was eerily calm, or else she was faking the hell out of it.

"Put the knife down, Rich," she said, as easily as if she were asking him to pass the butter dish. "You're upsetting the girls."

Then came the worst part for me, when I realized I had to go to the bathroom. The bathroom was just down the hall, but I was petrified to walk past my father, flat on his belly like a soldier in a foxhole, the knife in his fist with its blade gleaming.

In that insane situation, I remember Mom, in a voice of absolute sweet reason, saying, "Go on ahead, Laurie. Daddy won't hurt you. It's not you he's mad at. It's me."

Then she turned to my dad, and in the same oddly flat voice said, "Rich, Laurie has to go to the bathroom. Would you please tell her that it's okay?"

He said nothing, just stared at us with those blazing blue eyes. I inched toward the door, still crying, but couldn't bring myself to walk past him. I wet myself and my PJs, and something about the shame of that moment disturbed me even more than the violence.

So twice we left, and twice we came back. As they say, the third time is the charm.

The next day, we were goners.

=========== Animal Tails ===========

The Chicken Man

Among the most moving Funny Farm rescue stories concerns a complete stranger, who remains a mystery to this day.

We called him "the Chicken Man." He would show up at the farm every once in a while, unshaven, shabbily dressed, and always cradling one or two chickens under his arms. He wouldn't reveal his name or say where he got the chickens, usually white leghorns or Cornish Cross hens.

In every case, the birds were clearly unhealthy, with a poor gait, overgrown claws, and limp, grayish combs. I was reluctant to accept them, and very wary of the Chicken Man, who spoke in monosyllables, never looked me in the eye, and seemed uneasy even to be in my presence. He refused to answer questions about the birds. All he wanted was to hand them over and get the hell out of there.

But he never asked for anything in return, and I couldn't turn away those poor chickens, which were shedding feathers by the handful, a sign of high stress. They also had signs of parasites and looked like they were about to keel over and die. I had to isolate them in separate coops, as healthy chickens will sometimes turn on sick or weakened birds (the words "pecking order" really apply here). Quarantining the sick birds also protected the healthy flocks from unknown infections.

The Chicken Man's visits continued for a year or more. Whenever he showed up, I greeted him warmly, but no longer pressed him for details, and, eventually, I guess he decided he could trust me. He owned up to working in a poultry processing plant. Each time a bird escaped the assembly line, this unlikely Samaritan would grab it, put it under his coat, then slip out and stow it in his truck until the end of his shift. Then he would bring it to the Funny Farm, where it could live a long, happy life.

His story moved me almost to tears. This man was clearly a poor laborer. He worked a job in which he witnessed or engaged in slaughter every single day. But he also had love and compassion in his heart.

When I reached out to embrace him, he backed away, out of reach. I think the man had feared we would judge him for the things he had to do to earn his pay. Maybe he was afraid that his secret would come to light and he would be accused of theft for taking the birds.

Over time, he stopped coming, I don't know why. It's been a long time since I've seen the Chicken Man, but in my heart and memory, I think of him as a hero: a doer of good deeds, within his power. Isn't that about all we can ask of anyone, or ourselves?

Wherever he is now, I hope this good man is well and knows I think of him with respect.

3

What Doesn't Kill You

For a week, maybe two, there was no electricity in that little house in the woods. It was wintertime, and we were constantly huddled against each other, dressed in three and four layers of clothes, trying in vain to stay warm. Then Mr. Clark jerry-rigged a connection, running multiple extension cords from the tax office on the highway all the way back to our place—at least a quarter of a mile—a stopgap measure until we could get a proper line.

And just like that, light and heat.

Next, we got a secondhand fridge and an apartment-size, two-burner stove. Then came a washing machine that, in use, clanked and shook and practically traveled across the dirt floor in the tiny basement, shaking the whole house. Next, our plumbing was connected, with water coming from a well on the property. Now we were living large.

Before we had a single stick of furniture, Mom's brother, our wonderful, impractical Uncle John, brought down a stereo system and a stack of music tapes. While we listened to *Laverne & Shirley's Greatest Hits* and *Fonzie's Favorites* (or, begrudgingly, Mom's choice, *The Wonderful World of Robert Goulet*), I heard the grown-ups talking quietly in the kitchen. From the growly tone of Uncle

John's voice, I knew he was talking about our dad: "Say the word, Anne. Just say it. I'll put him in the river."

Uncle John was six-four and 260 pounds or more—the sweetest guy on earth in the body of the Incredible Hulk. He could have snapped my father in two like a Kit Kat.

"Leave it alone, John," Mom tutted. "Two wrongs don't make a right."

And that, in a nutshell, is my mother: she spoke in what could be considered platitudes, or clichés, or Hallmark-card sentiments:

"Every cloud has a silver lining."

"All's well that ends well."

"Don't cry over spilled milk."

"It's always darkest before the dawn."

She warned us not to put the cart before the horse, or all our eggs in one basket. She told us that patience is a virtue, virtue is its own reward, and honesty is the best policy. In her view, all these sayings summed up foundational truths.

Another one she must have learned from hard experience: "Don't put the key to your happiness in someone else's pocket." And then there's the saying she coined herself, which she would repeat to us again and again over the years. When you think about it, it makes no real sense, but it always cheered me up when I was unhappy, which I guess was the whole point:

"The more you cry, the less you'll pee."

Mom scared up some thrift-store furnishings, a frayed sofa and a few chairs along with a set of cookware and a box of dishes. And because she needed to have music, she found a castoff player piano and begged some guy friends to pick it up and lug it to our shack in the woods. It went a long way toward making the house feel like home.

But it was a truly miraculous day when our McNulty grandparents, Mom-Mom and Pop-Pop, drove down from Philadelphia, lugging a bulky console TV set, a black-and-white Magnavox complete with rabbit ears.

We plugged it in, it buzzed to life, and we gathered around it, almost as if we were warming ourselves around its cathode rays. We flipped the channels to see if we had any good ones, as our grandparents carted in sacks of groceries and started stocking the cabinet.

I glanced back, and for some reason felt embarrassed to see Pop-Pop press a wad of dollar bills into Mom's hand.

"Pride is a sin," he muttered in a gruff voice. "Take it, Anne."

I quickly looked back to the TV, where all families were happy and nothing went wrong that couldn't be easily mended. With the Bradys and the Partridges and the Cunninghams, I thought, life seemed tolerable again. Almost normal.

Sometimes at night, Mom would stand us around the piano in an old-fashioned family sing. One of her favorite tunes was a ditty from a 1940s musical called "A Shanty in Old Shanty Town." I can still hear her singing the lyrics, about that "tumbledown shack" in the pines, with a roof "so slanty, it touches the ground." To her, it was no less a home, despite its many flaws.

My memories of that time—my parents' final breakup and the falling apart of my family—are chaotic and incomplete. What I do remember, vividly, is the feeling of it all—a whole jumble of feelings: bewilderment, and betrayal, and divided loyalties, and the trauma of being ripped from one life and dropped headfirst into another.

If this could happen—if our loving parents could become enemies, and we could be exiled from our own home—then nothing in the world was trustworthy or safe. If this bad thing could befall us, what bad thing would happen next?

For many years, I had a recurring dream of being chased by a monster through a darkened house. Heart thudding, I would run through a maze of hallways and collide with undulating, formless walls. I would hear the creature's quickening footsteps right on my heels, and feel its hot breath on my neck.

In those dreams, my monster always had blue eyes, and fingers as bright and sharp as kitchen knives.

As terrifying as the dream was, I always broke free in the end. I would fling myself out a half-open door, escaping from that dark and shadowy maze into a brilliant landscape, flooded with color and light. And there in a clearing, a hot-air balloon would be waiting for me, and I'd hitch a ride, like Dorothy Gale on her way back to Oz.

In the new house, my mother was unwavering in her cheerfulness, at least when she knew we were watching. But sometimes I caught her crying at the kitchen sink, or guessed by her sniffly voice and swollen eyes that she'd allowed herself a little cry in the bathroom.

Years afterward, she confided that she had quietly broken down in those early months, and even seen a psychiatrist to try to keep from flying apart at the seams. And who could blame her? In terms of life experience, Mom was little more than a girl, a scared, unhappy girl in a jam, with three kids hanging on her neck and nowhere to turn for help. All the more remarkable, then, that she decided to take life the hard way and strike out on her own, rather than continue the sham of her marriage. When we complained, she told us "Suck it up." And she sure set the example.

========= Animal Tails =========

Three Little Pigs

Tens of thousands of children visit the Funny Farm each year, and we don't share full details of our animals' sad pasts because it could be upsetting for these young visitors. What we do tell them is that each of the animals living here is a rescue and each has found a home, a happy ending, and lots and lots of brothers and sisters.

Among them are three little pigs we call Papa, Bo, and Luke.

They were discovered by a woman searching for her lost dog in nearby Williamstown. Tramping through the woods, she came upon an abandoned shed, heard scratching sounds from within, and investigated. Inside, a family of pigs: three dead and three others barely alive, with no food and no water.

Immediately, she called New Jersey Aid for Animals, and Aid for Animals called the Funny Farm. (A shout-out here to the network of animal rescues here in South Jersey. They're fantastic, and each one supports all the others in their shared mission to help animals in need. If one organization can't help, it sends out an alert and soon the whole party line lights up until someone is able to lend a hand.)

I dropped everything and raced to Williamstown. What a terrible scene. The surviving animals—an adult male and two male piglets—had been without food for so long they ate the mom and two siblings just to survive. Even so, they were skeletal. I rushed them back to the Funny Farm and placed them in a specially built pig house with food, water, and clean straw and hay. I crossed my fingers for their recovery, and immediately called the vet, but they were in such bad shape. We all had our doubts that they would survive.

With animals that have been starved, it's important to reintroduce food slowly, serving them small meals several times a day until their bodies can handle more nutrition. These little piggies were so fearful that they wouldn't come out even at feeding times unless their human caretakers backed way off. I can only imagine how they were once treated.

We understood their apprehension—after all, it was people who had done this to them—and we gave them their space until they learned to trust us.

Eventually, they came out more and began eating more, snorting excitedly as they did so. I remember the great day I went out to the pig house and all three of them scuttled over to the fence, their short legs pumping and their corkscrew tails wagging happily. They were no longer afraid. That was the moment I knew they were going to be okay.

Pigs are very smart and clean animals. Although they love to play in the mud, they keep their sleeping areas clean. They are more intelligent than dogs and have wonderful memories. They don't have sweat glands, so mud isn't just fun for them, it keeps them cool. Pigs are also very social and love the company of volunteers and visitors and each other, sometimes napping with their friends.

I wish we could have saved the poor mother and the other piglets. I sure as hell wish the person who left them to die had been found and punished. But it's enough to know that Papa, Bo, and Luke will live out their days in peace and security at the Funny Farm, where kids can see and appreciate them as they are, untroubled by their sad past.

4

Accidentally Eden

People often ask me how I started the Funny Farm. My answer is always the same: Not on purpose. As you'll see, the same was true of my mother.

It soon became clear that the teenagers who used to hang out at the house in the woods wouldn't surrender it without a fight. This had been their crash pad, their very own Love Shack, and we had invaded it, spoiling their fun. So they decided to try to reclaim their turf by vandalizing the place, burglarizing it, and scaring the bejesus out of us.

They must have watched our comings and goings, because when we weren't home, they broke in and hauled off the TV our grandparents had been kind enough to give us. When my grandparents replaced the TV, they stole the replacement. They raided the kitchen, broke the plates and cups, overturned the furniture, and generally trashed the place we'd spent so much time putting into a semblance of order. When my mother put dead bolts on the doors, they broke in through the windows.

Mom was a tough cookie, and brave, but these incidents really unstrung her. Our house was off the beaten track, set back from the highway, among the trees and completely hidden from view. If those hoodlums wanted to hurt us, they could do so at their leisure and be gone before anyone was the wiser. She started watching anxiously at the windows, unnerved to know that, somewhere out there, someone was watching back. The house was ransacked six times before she had that lightbulb moment, the moment that changed all our lives.

"Kids," she said, gathering us together one night, "what do you think about us getting a dog? I know you've always wanted one, and there's no better security system."

A dog of our very own!

Of course we said yes, jumping for joy at the prospect.

"Good," Mom said, with a thoughtful look. "I know just the one."

With no child support or alimony, and with minimal work history, she had taken a series of odd jobs—low-paying, menial, manual labor—just to keep us fed and housed. She stuffed envelopes, earning two cents apiece. She stocked shelves and swept floors at the MAB paint store out on the highway. The onetime lady of leisure now cleaned houses, and I wonder if this was particularly demoralizing for her, to scrub floors and toilets or wash and fold laundry for women who months earlier might have been on the same church committee or at the same bridge table.

Her main job, though, was cleaning cages at the local Animal Control. This wasn't an animal shelter or the SPCA, but a local agency that picked up animals of all kinds, including injured wildlife, "nuisance" animals that got into people's attics or gardens, and stray cats and dogs.

Animal Control sometimes found new homes for adoptable pets, and in the cases of so-called pests, like bats or squirrels, occasionally relocated them back to the wild. But all too often, it was the last stop for these creatures, which were quickly euthanized.

Working there, Mom discovered something that must have been inside her all along: an instinctive, deep-down care for those poor discarded animals. Like dogs that were given as birthday or Christmas presents, and weren't wanted when they were no longer cute and puppyish. And pets of all kinds whose owners had died or gone into nursing homes, and had no one left to love them. And pet rabbits, turned loose to survive on their own, that now would have to be destroyed. And cats that had been allowed to breed until they were bred out, only to end up on the kill list, along with their kittens.

It was an endless litany of sad stories. Many nights Mom came home brooding about some poor thing—someone's family member, someone's best friend, who because of inconvenience or whim or hardship or indifference had been turned over to Animal Control and stuck in a cage with a cold concrete floor.

Within days, she knew, these misfits would be gone. Sometimes she almost wished they would be put to sleep more quickly, to end their anguish. She knew what it was like to be abandoned, and the sad and frightened faces behind those bars haunted her.

But this is where she found the solution to our vandalism problem, as well as a whole new way of life. Someone had surrendered a handsome German shepherd who would become her first rescue and our faithful guardian.

We were beside ourselves with excitement the day she brought home Wolf. Showering him with hugs and kisses, we wondered what on earth could have made his former family give up this magnificent animal.

"Did you know German shepherds are also called police dogs?" Mom asked us. "Wolf will keep those roughnecks away. He'll just know that it's his job to defend us."

Sure enough, Wolf took immediate command of the home front and patrolled the edges of our property as if he were on a watchtower. He was extremely protective of us kids and trailed behind us whenever we played outside. Nothing got by his masterful nose and booming bark.

Way out in front of our property, at the foot of the path leading back to the house, Mom posted a hand-lettered sign saying, "Beware! Attack Dog on Duty!" She stuck on a picture of a snarling, monstrous dog with pointed yellow teeth and foaming jaws. I had to laugh. With his new family, Wolf was a pussycat, but I had no doubt he would have turned into a fierce protector if someone tried to harm us.

Wolf would soon be joined by Erin, a sleek and silky Irish setter, and Georgie, a big, galumphing English sheepdog pup. This trio was just the start. Soon it was no surprise to see Mom walk in the door with all kinds of animals, wild and tame, big and small: raccoons and squirrels, possums and puppies—even sheep, goats, and pigs. It was about this time that she started referring to our house as the Funny Farm.

"Look what followed me home," she would joke, walking in with a skunk in her arms. "Can I keep him?"

As I said, it wasn't on purpose. It was the happiest accident ever.

For a while, those teenage thugs would still roar up to the house in their car, shout profanities, and toss rocks. But then Wolf would go powering after them, barking at the top of his lungs. Eventually, the boys gave up—or grew up, as the case may be. The break-ins ended. We were no longer a target, at least not for them.

With a coat of paint on the inside walls and throw rugs on the floor and hand-sewn curtains in the windows and every corner scrubbed clean, our new house was what Mom had promised it would be: nice and cozy, or pretty near to it.

But cozy, in this case, was just another word for cramped. Mom's bed was a pull-out sofa in the living room, meaning she had zero privacy, except a curtain on rings that she drew each night at bedtime. As for Stephen, well, it's a good thing he was easy-going, because she shoved a bed into a room no bigger than a walk-in closet (optimistically, she called it "the sewing room"), and that's where he slept.

There was no privacy about bathing, either, and if we had any sense of modesty, we got over it in a hurry. The bathroom had a sliding pocket door with no lock, and it was always crowded, with one of us in the tub, one of us on the toilet, and one of us brushing their teeth at the cracked mirror over the sink. I envied Stephen, who would usually go outside to pee. If it was too cold, no wor-ries: he could just stand at the back door, aim, and fire. We girls were far more fastidious, though in a pinch I wasn't above dashing out to the nearest clump of trees.

Despite our protests, Cathy and I were stuck together in the single bedroom, fighting over our territory in a secondhand dou-ble bed. Cathy complained that I kicked at night. I complained that Cathy hogged the covers. We both complained that the other one snored. My doll Penny's "waa, waa" sound drove her nuts.

But some things we agreed on. Because Mom worked at the MAB store—right down the highway, close enough so she could walk—paint came cheap. Together, my sister and I chose a laven-der tint for the walls and a deeper, violet hue for the ceiling. It was pretty. But we were still two grouchy peas in a very small pod. Cathy's side of the room was tidy, with the next day's clothes neatly folded on a chair, schoolbooks tucked in her schoolbag, and the bag hanging on a hook on the door, just so.

My side was chaos—jeans and T-shirts and mud-encrusted shoes in piles on the floor, paints, colored pencils, and other art supplies cluttering every surface, and the pictures I had drawn hap-hazardly tacked up on the walls.

For as long as I could remember, I had loved to draw, and had shown a gift for it that Mom actively encouraged. When one of my kindergarten masterpieces—a farm with animals, naturally—won an award, my teacher, Mrs. Ebbecke, said it was the first time she'd seen a kindergartener draw with a sense of perspective.

I didn't understand what perspective was, not in a theoretical or practical way, yet I'd seen my subjects as dimensional, and was able to draw them that way. Mom pasted my landscape to a piece of wood, shellacked it until it could have survived an A-bomb, and hung it on the living room wall. My first gallery piece.

Whenever I wasn't outside playing, I could be found bent over a sketch pad, drawing frolicking animals and houses with happy people in the windows. I aspired to be like Harold, the hero of the children's storybook *Harold and the Purple Crayon*. Armed with his trusty crayon, the round-headed little boy had only to draw something to make it appear. When there's no moon, he draws one and then hangs it in the sky. When there's nowhere to walk, he traces a pathway that leads him to a hill, then a forest, then a mountain. He has many adventures, and all of his adventures lead him safely back home.

To me, this was a magical idea. Like Harold, I would draw the world the way I wanted it to be: safe and peaceful, green and abundant, filled with animals and a place to come home to. In my mind, and in the pages of my sketchbook, I must have designed this world a thousand times.

I also drew dark, stormy nights and sharp-clawed, blue-eyed monsters. But only the happy scenes went up on the wall. All the others I stashed in a folder under the bed.

For a while, I thought of the little house in the woods as another way station, temporary, like one of the motels where we used to hide out from Dad. I needed to think of it as short-term, just to tolerate being there. But six months went by, then seven, then a year, and it dawned on me: this was it. Be it ever so humble.

The dirt road that led from the highway to the house was like a washboard, so uneven it could knock the hubcaps off a car. In dry weather it was like a dust bowl back there, and in the rain, it flooded so much we felt like we were surrounded by a moat. We still didn't have any front steps, and the view from the living room window was that mountain of trash next door.

But Mom did what she could to make the place more home-like, transforming it from a beat-up squatter's shack to a quaint woodland cottage—or so she repeatedly said. A collector at heart, she covered every surface with knickknacks, trinkets, and tchotchkes. She crowded the walls with framed photos, more of the kids' artwork, and landscapes she'd picked out of other people's trash. She festooned the ceiling with cut-out moons, planets, and stars that glowed in the dark. She even had that epitome of kitsch, a velvet Elvis painting.

If any of us griped about our new digs—and we did, a lot—she would chide us, loud and long, for our ingratitude. "You have a roof over your heads, don't you? You have food on the table, simple as it is, don't you? There are people in this world whose families will go to bed hungry tonight, who would give their eyes to have what you three take for granted. So suck it up.

"When you get a real problem, let me know."

In addition to the house, Mom transformed herself, and for me, it was like watching someone take off an elaborate costume. First went the lacquered nails and the fancy dresses. Then the Tammy

Wynette bouffant and Tammy's "stand-by-your-man" attitude. Her hair went from platinum blonde to a tumble of wavy brown curls, until she looked like a teenager again. She traded miniskirts for jeans and sneaks or cowboy boots. Her creamy-white hands grew red and rough, and if she got dirt under her nails, well, it was all in a day's work.

I had adored my mom as a glamour-puss, but she was even prettier without the window dressing. One thing she never gave up, though, and that was makeup. Mom firmly believed that lipstick, blush, and a touch of mascara always made a bad situation better. When Cathy and I got older, any time we went into a funk she would say, "Go put on a little lipstick. You'll feel better."

Undoubtedly, there were people in the country-club and cocktail-party set who thought Mom lost everything when her marriage ended.

But from where I stand—where my sister and brother stand— she found more than she lost. She found it in herself to say, "Enough." She found the tenacity—that inner *something*—that kept her keeping on. She found she didn't need to be upper class or rich to have a meaningful, useful, and wonderful life.

None of it happened fast or in a straight line. I was there, and saw her wander down dead-end streets and blunder in relationships all her life. But when she took off that costume, a truer self was underneath, something rock solid that lasted through it all.

As Annie Oakley put it, in Annie McNulty's favorite musical:

> *"Got no diamond, got no pearl,*
> *Still I think I'm a lucky girl.*
> *I've got the sun in the morning*
> *And the moon at night."*

Animal Tails

Emily the Emu

Emily the emu began her life as a science project.

A local teacher, the wife of one of my work colleagues, had conducted a classroom experiment to hatch two emu eggs. It was kind of a head-scratcher to me. Did she think she was getting ordinary classroom pets, like hamsters or goldfish? What did she plan to do with the birds once they grew to their full height and weight (up to six and a half feet and 120 pounds)? Did she know that emus, the second-largest birds in the world next to ostriches, can do serious injury with their massive, three-toed feet? Besides all that, owning an emu is not a short-term commitment: in captivity these exotic birds, which are native to the Australian savanna, can live thirty-five years or more.

At any rate, it was an interesting project for schoolchildren. Both eggs hatched, and the teacher named them Emily and Enoch.

As the birds grew, the teacher moved them to the yard of her home in rural Cape May County, in the southernmost part of New Jersey. Soon enough, they found out that Emily was a wanderer, prone to taking off down residential streets and roads, scaring the pants off the townspeople. And just try lassoing an angry emu. Those goofy-looking, gangly birds, which look like something out of *Jurassic Park*, can kick out with those powerful legs like Jackie Chan. The toe barbs of emus "are capable of eviscerating animals," according to the *Encyclopedia Britannica* (which reassuringly adds that "human fatalities are extremely rare").

I was playing volleyball as part of a work league and heard someone say, "Hey, farm girl, how about taking on a couple of emus?" Soon I found myself the proud owner of Emily and Enoch.

Enoch was a homebody, pretty placid, a lover boy; he'd stand at the pasture fence, batting his big hazel eyes and waiting to be fed and petted. Emily was a loner and alas, didn't give up her roving ways after she moved to the Funny Farm. One time, a storm blew through, felling a tree that in turn broke her pasture fence. Emily took off like Papillon, and was gone for two full months.

Her escape made the news, and we got constant updates from confused people who said, "I swear I'm not drunk, but I just saw a six-foot turkey in my backyard!"

Eventually Emily ended up at the Buena Vista Campground, about six miles way. Somehow, the folks there got her to a fenced-in area, and I went to retrieve her. As I approached, she bobbed and weaved and made the emu's characteristic drumming sound, meaning she was mighty peeved. The feathers of her long neck rose up in a sign of pure rage. I had to slip a sock over her head and bind her muscular legs together to get her into the truck and back home. It almost felt like all I needed was a white van to feel like a gangster girl kidnapper.

Enoch, always on the sickly side, only lived about ten years. We took in another emu called Elvis, who has since left the building, too. Sometimes on my tours, I say Emily is a black widow, because she has outlived two husbands.

— 5 —

Going for Broke

Once we were settled in the woods, it was pretty quick work for Dad to find out where we were living. Soon he showed up on the doorstep, hat in hand, begging Mom to come back and give their marriage another try.

He wrung his hands. He swore that he loved her. He confessed that he'd strayed and promised to walk the line. He even teared up a little as he gazed at her with those Paul Newman eyes.

But beneath his contrition—it would have been imperceptible to anyone who didn't know him—was the old swagger, the cocky assurance that he could get around her, win her back, and gull her into thinking he would change.

The letter from the girlfriend's mother had been the crowning humiliation, and the final straw was yet another letter, this one with a photo enclosed: Dad celebrating the holidays with a strange woman and her children. All of them smiling, with a Christmas tree topped with a star in the background.

Because of those things and the unspeakable violence of our final days at home, Mom knew her marriage was finished. It was like a door had slammed and locked tight. She couldn't have opened it again if she wanted to. Cathy felt the same way. She gladly would have never seen our father again.

I felt differently. For all that I'd seen and heard, after all the beatings and even the bloodletting, I still loved my dad. I feared him, but I loved him and missed him. If I had any anger it had gone underground, like an animal that burrows deep into the earth, to stay safe.

Maybe it had something to do with my resemblance to him. Cathy was the image of our mom, with her wavy brown hair and fair complexion. She had the same sparkling Irish eyes, the same softly rounded chin and cheeks. I was almost a carbon copy of Dad, with poker-straight blonde hair, pale, pinkish skin, and a toothy smile. To fully escape him, I would have had to stop looking in mirrors. Stephen, too, favored Dad's side of the family. And just like me, he missed our father.

I found myself searching for reasons to forgive Dad, or at least grade him on a curve. From bits of grown-up talk, I had deduced that he, too, had grown up in a violent home, and had been repeatedly, cruelly beaten by his father, Chick. If such things truly are passed from generation to generation, my father hadn't escaped his legacy.

Of course, as a little kid, all I really wanted was the feeling of safety, the cocoon feeling I knew when things were good between my parents, when she would sing love songs at parties, just for him. I must say I admire her for not badmouthing our father, despite all she had been through. It took time for her to get there after our escape—a good long time, as much as a year—but after that she urged us to maintain some kind of relationship with Dad if we wanted to.

"Go see him. He's your father, he loves you," she would say. "This was never about him not loving you."

In light of everything that followed, I have to wonder.

In those days, a man with money, lawyers, and influence—and our dad had all three, in abundance—could sometimes skate by without financially supporting his children. Our father earned more than $80,000 a year—about $400,000 today, what with his professorship, his investments, and what he made dabbling in the stock market. But he refused to pay a dime toward our support.

Mom lifted her chin in that pugnacious Irish way and said, "I don't need his money. I just want to be free." She wouldn't apply for any kind of public assistance. Between her jobs at Animal Control and the hardware store and the endless stuffing and stamping of envelopes, she made ends meet, barely.

Eventually, Dad's wages were attached: Mom was awarded ten dollars per child, per week. The support payment was later tripled, to $360 a month. And that's when he challenged her for custody.

Dad didn't really want us. Mom knew it. I'm pretty certain the family courts knew it. In our hearts, Cathy, Stephen, and I knew it. Even so, we were hauled into court on what seemed like a monthly basis, quizzed by weary-looking advocates and judges who asked which parent we wanted to live with. Every time, without hesitation, we said the same thing: "Mom." But the matter was never settled, and the custody battle dragged on for years, like *Family Feud*, but for real and on endless repeat.

Mom appealed to her parish priest for help, but he told her to go back home where she belonged. "Strive to be a better wife," he intoned, "so Richard will be inspired to be a better husband."

That was the end of church for Mom. She retained custody of the kids, and Dad got custody of God.

The family court eventually ordered that we kids spend part of each weekend at Dad's. As much as we had missed our old life—or at least the *things* of that life, the comforts, the roomy rooms and piles of toys—it was unsettling to be wrenched back into it, the place we remembered as a battleground. Weekends are supposed to be fun, relaxing, a kid's time off. Now we were sentenced to spend them with Dad, a man we were afraid to trust.

As soon as we got to Timber Heights Court, he'd march us to our rooms to take off our smelly farm clothes, then order us to scrub our dirty necks, clean under our nails, and change into "decent" clothes so we could rejoin civilization.

Not that we didn't have good times; we did, at the zoo and the park, and especially at our big house on the bay in Wildwood Crest, hitting the beach by day and the boardwalk at night, using rolls of paper tickets to go on all the amusement park rides (I rode everything but the Ferris wheel, because I was petrified of heights).

But it was the kind of organized fun you might have at a friend's birthday party or school picnic, a behaving, obedient, inside-the-lines kind of fun, with lots of rules. We had to be up no later than eight in the morning and sit down for dinner precisely at five-thirty in the evening. We could ride our bikes for no more than an hour, and were allowed ninety minutes of TV time at night. At Dad's house, being a kid was like punching a time card. God forbid one of us got a dirty face. It was so unlike our free-range lives at the farm.

On the longer weekends, we'd troop off to Sunday mass, neatly dressed and pressed, with Dad leading the procession. His fellow parishioners seemed to feel for him, the poor man whose wife had abandoned him and taken their little ones. I remember their eyes on us, curious, pitying, and, I suspect, filled with judgment.

I'm reminded by photographs taken at Dad's around this time that I always kept a hand on his forearm, lightly but possessively, as if to keep him from vanishing into air.

They say kids are adaptable, and in the case of Cathy, Stephen, and me, it sure was true. Poverty eventually became background, as routine to us as the boiled spaghetti we ate at least four times a week. (Stephen got so sick of it, he eventually swore off spaghetti and consumed nothing but peanut butter and jelly sandwiches for years—for breakfast, lunch, and dinner.)

And there were compensations to our new life, compensations that were rich and unexpected. As I've said, the house was on seven wooded acres with an orchard out back and rows and rows of trees, half apple, half peach. Not all of it belonged to Mr. Clark, our landlord, but it wasn't fenced off in any way, so as far as we were concerned, that made it ours—a kingdom of endless discovery, teeming with wild things: foxes and beavers, chipmunks and groundhogs, hawks and owls.

"Squatters' rights," said Mom.

We basically claimed the whole property as our own.

Most times when she wasn't working, Mom was too bushed to keep us entertained, and she detested seeing us parked in front of the TV set. So she'd throw open the back door and turn us loose. "Out," she would say. "And don't show your faces around here until suppertime."

We never tired of wandering those woods and spotting the telltale signs of animals that lived right alongside us, but mostly were hidden from sight. We learned to identify different paw prints and nests and even piles of scat. We learned that a flattened section of grass meant a deer had bedded down there. We discovered that bark peeled away from a tree meant that that same deer or some other animal had rubbed against it to scratch an itch or mark its territory.

We built a makeshift firepit out of stones and gravel, piled a couple of old sofas and chairs in a semicircle around it, and built bonfires all year long. At last, we got our fair share of s'mores.

In spring and summer, the place burst into life. Fields of wildflowers drew the birds and bees and hummingbirds. A grove of milkweed attracted monarch butterflies, sometimes by the hundreds. In the fall when the spiny milkweed pods opened, it was a miracle to me to see their silken seeds fill the air, floating around us like angels or tiny parachutes.

We turned into wild things ourselves, barefoot and free, almost feral. We never cared how dirty or unkempt we got, because we had fun.

We worked hard and played harder. We slept like stones, on nature's clock—slumbering when the sun went down and waking at dawn to the crowing of roosters. We charged nonstop through every day, swimming in the swimming hole, climbing trees, building tree forts, and swinging from vines like howler monkeys. We caught tadpoles in mason jars and watched as they miraculously turned into frogs. On summer nights, the fireflies came out, winking on and off in the darkness like little polka dots. We caught them in jars, too, then dove under the covers to see if we could read by their light.

When it was hot, we thought nothing of running half-naked through our woods or riding bikes in the spray of crop-dusting planes that dive-bombed our orchard.

The fruit was divine. The peaches were covered with a quarter-inch of fuzz, enough to make your palms itchy, but they were astonishingly sweet, delicious and drippy with juice. We collected windfall fruits for pie, to feed the pigs, or just to use as missiles—the riper the better, so they would splatter on impact. Stephen had a particularly good pitching arm.

Many years later, we would find out that our swimming hole had been contaminated by a cesspool on the grounds, and the crop dusters had been dumping clouds of pure pesticides. It didn't matter. Though we hardly ever saw a doctor—because no insurance—we were as strong and sturdy as mountain goats, running behind the orchard sprayers and dancing in showers of DDT.

When we got over the shock of being uprooted from our former, privileged life, we realized with surprise that we were pretty darned happy.

================= Animal Tails =================

Debbie De Goose

People ask how I can remember the names of more than six hundred animals, especially when there are dozens of a single species. One white goose looks like every other white goose, right?

At first glance, maybe they do all look alike. But each animal has different behaviors, a distinct personality, and sometimes, a distinguishing deformity. At the Funny Farm, you'll see dozens of ducks and geese roving the property, many with a defect called "angel wing." This condition causes the flight feathers of a bird's wings to twist away from its body. The deformity looks uncomfortable, but doesn't hurt. However, it does keep birds from flying, which means they can't escape predators. In the wild, these poor creatures don't live long, but our angel-wing crew, while permanently grounded, is safe.

One of them is Debbie De Goose—and there's no mistaking Debbie for any other bird. Along with the angel-wing that afflicts so many of our feathered friends, Debbie also has bright blue eyes, a bossy manner, an imperious strut, and a story for everyone! Found as an orphaned gosling, Debbie lived several months with an older woman who treated her like a lapdog. When the woman became ill, she reached out to the Funny Farm, hoping we could take her pampered pet. After Debbie joined our family, instead of falling in with the other geese, she chose to join the dog pack. It was comical to see the dogs dashing around the farm with a strutting, honking goose in their midst. So you can see, it's easy to pick Debbie out of a crowd.

While Debbie's a bit of a prima donna, she really loves people—and for a time, developed a special passion for one of our delivery drivers.

His name was Steve, and he worked for UPS, Mom's former employer. Well, Debbie developed a mad crush on Steve. Every day, as soon as he pressed the electric panel to open the gate, she'd go hurtling in his direction, madly flapping her wings and squawking at the top of her lungs. One day, when a female driver showed up instead, Debbie was fit to be tied.

The romance of Debbie and the UPS driver blew up when one of our volunteers posted it on social media, calling the driver "Dreamie Stevie" and saying, "he has a smile big enough to light up a chicken coop!" Speaking in Debbie's "voice," the social media volunteer went on and on about Stevie, describing how she couldn't wait for his next visit. The posts captured national attention with Debbie's dizzy attitude, her bossy manner, and her absolute passion for the delivery guy, all true stories based on her real behavior. He wrote in her voice, "Don't tell Stevie I am his secret admirer!"

Oops! Steve's wife saw the post, and thought it was *me* proclaiming my love for her husband. Hastily, I assured her that this was not the case, it was my social media volunteer speaking in the goose's voice, just doing his job. Months later, I heard most of the women on his route began calling him "Dreamie Stevie!" I noticed the name brought a big smile to his face.

The silly story of the goose and the delivery driver was shared far and wide, and UPS executives at the national level thought it was hilarious. But the local branch didn't share their enthusiasm. When a photo was posted of Steve holding Debbie and standing in the door of his truck, his bosses became upset and said he had broken the rules. Conduct unbecoming a UPS driver, although it was the most viewed photo on UPSdogs.com.

Who knows why certain animals become enamored with certain people—or things? Another Funny Farm goose, Henry, loves to chase cars, flying at eye level with the driver and honking insistently. At night, he sleeps next to my car. Go figure.

As you can see, animals are very different and when you live with them every day, you don't really see them as part of a crowd, but as individuals, special in their own way.

6

Mayonnaise Sandwiches

There was no shortage of hard-luck cases at Animal Control, and dozens of those cases found their way to the Funny Farm. Every time I turned around, the menagerie seemed to grow, two by two, four by four, as if Noah had parked his ark in the woods near Turnersville, dropped the tailgate, and said, "Welcome home."

Dad had never let us keep pets at Timber Heights Court, with the exception of Spooky. And now we had a surplus: dogs, cats, chickens, roosters, geese, and even a pair of raccoons we called Randy and Rocky.

South Jersey was a lot more countrified then, and it wasn't uncommon for Animal Control to pick up goats and sheep running loose along the Black Horse Pike. Mom took them in, too.

Mr. Clark knew all about it, but he must have been the most laid-back landlord ever. As long as he got his hundred bucks a month, we could have raised alligators back there and he would have just shrugged. He was freewheeling that way. Down the dirt path closer to the highway, he let space to a bunch of college guys who lived out of a double-wide mobile home. They were long-haired and unkempt, foulmouthed and a little on the wild side, but pretty nice all the same. Young as he was, Stephen fell in with that rowdy crowd like a mascot, and on weekends would hang out with the guys as they chugged beers and roasted hot dogs.

Just like camping.

The health spa on the property was also a jumping place. From what I could tell, it got more traffic than the insurance office, the tax man, and the Hitcharama combined. All day long, the lines formed—truckers and construction workers, store clerks and business types—for "healing shiatsu," "deep-tissue therapy," and "integrative bodywork."

Each morning as I walked to the bus, I waved to the girls who worked there, all of them young and leggy with flowing hair, in micro-miniskirts and formfitting tops. To a one, they were beautiful, and just as nice as our bonfire guys.

"Nice for a price," said Mom cryptically, who referred to the place as Afternoon Delight. I had no idea what that meant, I just knew the girls were pretty and kind to me, and I thought it wouldn't be too bad to grow up just like them, so pretty and popular.

It would be years before I figured out that the health spa was a massage parlor, and not the legitimate kind.

That summer we discovered that a piglet was running wild in the peach orchard behind our house. Maybe she was a fugitive from another farm, or an escapee from a livestock truck. For weeks, we tried to run her to ground, but she was cagey, quick, and, to our surprise, as nimble as a jackrabbit. Soon we began to worry that she would starve or be set upon by one of the hawks or eagles that circled lazily above the treetops.

Finally, Mom turned for help to her pals at Animal Control, who sent out an agent with a tranquilizer gun. He quickly bagged our elusive quarry. We named her Priscilla, and in six months she went from a naked, squealing pink piglet—like an oversize dime bank—to a snuffling, snorting, bristly-backed 200-pounder. That was just the beginning of Priscilla. Ultimately, she grew to more than 1,500 pounds, so big that Stephen, Cathy, and I could ride her like a pony.

Priscilla taught me that pigs aren't low, filthy creatures, as some people believe, but sensitive, smart, affectionate, and quite finicky about their living quarters. Sure, they roll around in the mud and dirt, but only to repel gnats and flies or keep their skin from getting sunburnt.

And although pigs can live on slop—as in any old garbage, including restaurant waste—Priscilla was quite the connoisseur. She loved her leafy greens and hay and fresh fruits, and I did my best to accommodate her. She was somehow dainty, with her flat pink snout and curlicue tail, and she began to star prominently in my artwork.

Priscilla also taught me that having animals isn't nonstop fun. For example, pigs—like all farm animals—need their hooves, nails, tusks, and even their teeth trimmed regularly. Imagine climbing into a pen with a hog the size of a Buick and trying to clip her overgrown nails, or filing the ends of a horse's molars. Mom learned how to do all these things from livestock manuals, then taught us. Needless to add, over the years, taking care of farm animals left us all with lasting scars.

It's clear my mother had a heart for animals, but she wasn't completely sentimental about them. She ate meat. So did Cathy and Stephen. For weeks, after living on spaghetti in all its ho-hum variations—spaghetti plain, spaghetti with Ragu, spaghetti with Alfredo sauce, and back to spaghetti plain—she would finally send one of our chickens to the local butcher. Vegetarianism was seen as faddish in those days, and most people would have been hard put to define the word.

I cried quarts when one of our flock was turned into a fryer, but Mom was unmoved. "Laurie, we gave that animal a happy life. Now that animal is giving us food. Fair exchange."

"Mom," I sobbed, "we can't eat our own pets!"

"We can't live on a steady diet of noodles, either. You're mad now, but when we have fried chicken for supper, you'll get glad."

I didn't get glad, then or ever. Ever since the night my father tried to force-feed me that rubbery steak, the very thought of eating meat had turned my stomach. So any time one of the farm animals ended up on the dinner table I would go hungry, or else have a mayonnaise sandwich: white bread and Hellmann's.

But it had to be Hellmann's. A couple of times, Mom got the cheap mayo and put it in the Hellmann's jar, thinking she could fool me. One whiff of it, and I would squawk, "Mom, please! Only the *real* mayonnaise!"

Every morning before school, it was Cathy's and my shared responsibility to feed the animals and milk the goats. Everyone in the family drank goat's milk; it was all we had, but none of us liked it—we thought it tasted too gamey, like a barnyard in a glass. Other people loved it, though, and used it to make butter and cheese. We started making extra money selling the milk and cream, along with dozens of chicken and duck eggs. Our own little cottage industry.

Mom would sometimes sell the goat kids, too, and you can be sure there were a lot of tears on those days. It was heartbreaking to see little members of our family carted off, bleating pitifully on the back of a truck, crying for their mamas. I wanted to say goodbye, but I was a coward. I would run into the woods and clamp my hands over my ears until the truck pulled away.

On those nights, after Cathy drifted off to sleep, I would climb down from my side of the bed, hit my knees, and ask God to make sure that, wherever those babies were, they would be taken care of and loved as I had loved them.

I couldn't bear to imagine any other outcome.

One mind-boggling afternoon, Mom walked in the door carrying a tiny foal, thin and knobby-kneed with legs like stilts, peeking from the depths of a coarse woolen blanket. He was a deep reddish-brown color—a bay, Mom called him—with dark ears, a black mane and tail, and one white leg.

A horse in the house! It was unbelievable. We rushed to see and play with him, but Mom shooed us away. He had a fractured foreleg, she explained. This was a critical injury for a horse, whose comparatively slender legs have to hold up a great big body.

Most of the time, horses with broken legs are put down—even million-dollar horses like Barbaro, who won the Kentucky Derby but shattered a leg running the Preakness; and the filly, Ruffian, who broke her ankle at Belmont Park. Thoroughbreds of that caliber are usually euthanized by injection, but in many cases, it's considered merciful to handle the job with dispatch: one quick bullet to the head. When the injured foal was brought into Animal Control, Mom had to beg her bosses not to shoot him on sight.

"Give me a chance to rehabilitate him," she implored. "If I can't nurse him back to health, I swear to God, I'll shoot him myself."

By this time, she had become quite friendly with Charlie and Judy, a couple who ran the local feed store. Charlie, the son and grandson of farmers, was astonishingly well-informed about animal care, and from him Mom learned the right way to splint and wrap the injured leg so it would have a shot at healing.

After that, it was all about getting the little colt stronger. That meant hand-feeding him from a bottle every couple of hours, day and night. I'll never forget the sight of my mother cradling him in her arms like a big baby as he latched onto the bottle's rubber nipple, his big eyes like black-agate marbles, shining up at her with unbridled love.

And he lived. Mom named him Shannon O'Leary, because his birthday was on March 17, St. Patrick's Day. For a month or more, he lived inside the house with us, and you can imagine we had zero luck trying to housebreak a horse.

Once again, we learned that having animals isn't always fun. We kids were on constant poop patrol, following Shannon with a dustpan and a scoop. We would pick up clods of manure, toss them out into the garden, then frantically scrub the floors and air out the small rooms.

When he finally got his legs under him, Mom started taking Shannon outside, where he graduated from uncertain hobbling to trotting and then cantering. Mom looked on, hands clasped, as nervous as if she were watching her child ride a two-wheeler for the first time. And it really was a sight to see. I'll never forget the first time Shannon took off across our field, then turned in circles and kicked up his heels, whinnying for pure joy. Mom let out a whoop, and everybody joined in.

He would grow from that bony little foal into a magnificent stallion—spirited, cantankerous, and, quite frankly, a bit of a jerk, probably because he was never gelded. Mom could ride him, but he seldom let anyone else aboard. I tried, swinging myself onto his broad back and clinging to his mane, but he would deliberately run under a low tree branch to scrape me off. Then he would look back over his shining hindquarters and regard me with what I felt sure was amused contempt.

As he grew, Shannon would break out to go see other horses—

lady horses that lived on other farms along the pike, who must have been sending pheromones on the wind. You couldn't blame him. He was a big, strapping boy, ready for love. But bringing him back was a monumental pain. I seldom missed a day of school unless we had to round up Shannon, sometimes chasing him in our car. There he would be, out in front, streaking down the four-lane at a full gallop, with Mom behind the wheel in hot pursuit and us kids in the back seat, hanging out the windows on either side, whooping and hollering like the cowboys on *Bonanza*.

To keep him safe at home, we finally got what amounted to a leash—a long, heavy chain attached to a pair of old truck tires. It gave Shannon plenty of space to roam and graze, but ensured that he couldn't escape the farm. Mom would drive a wooden stake into the ground near a nice grassy patch—painted pink, so it would stand out—and let him feed there for a while, then rotate him all over the property.

Despite his fiery temperament—Shannon was a biter and a hairpuller—I loved him, in part because he was so beautiful, with his gleaming russet coat and rippling mane and tail, and also because of his stallion spirit.

Stephen felt otherwise. He resented Shannon's horseplay, and one winter day, made the mistake of coming up behind him and hitting him with a snowball. Shannon's vengeance was swift and certain. He turned, lowered his head like a bull, and charged, propelling Stephen into a barbed-wire fence. Then he flipped him over like a rag doll and tried to take a chunk out of his back.

Stephen scrambled to his feet, shrieking, and went running in to Mom. "Shannon bit me!" He pulled up his shirt. The red bite marks were visible, even though he had been wearing a heavy jacket.

Mom knew Shannon could be a naughty horse, but she also knew that Stephen liked to provoke him. "What did you do?" she asked.

He looked sullen. "Nothing."

More sternly now. *"What did you do to Shannon?"*

Stephen gulped back tears. "Hit him with a snowball."

Mom returned to her chores. "Serves you right."

Eventually, we had more horses: Goldie, then Callie, then Mom's darling, an inky black mare she called Nancy. Sometimes if the car was out of commission, Mom would use Nancy to run errands or even go to her job at the paint store, and "park" her in the parking lot, along with a feedbag and a couple of apples.

Not surprisingly, Mom acquired a reputation around town as the local animal lady—a term that was sometimes prefaced with the word "crazy."

I admit, sometimes I found her antics the tiniest bit embarrassing, and wished she would behave more like other kids' mothers. Other times, I suspected I had the coolest mom on the planet.

========== **Animal Tails** ==========

Juliet

Unlike the trio of pigs found starving in the woods, Juliet came in with the opposite problem. Bought as a pet, she was overfed to the point of obesity, until she tipped the scales at 450 pounds. (Her ideal weight is 250 pounds.)

Julie was sold to her unsuspecting owners as a "mini-pig"—a misleading label if there ever was one. Mini-pigs—also called micro-pigs and teacup pigs—don't stay small unless you underfeed them, which, I'm sorry to say, some breeders do in order to sell them. But give them a regular diet, and boom, they sort of explode.

Julie's family planned to keep her inside the house, like a

dog—again, believing she'd stay cute and cuddly—and then proceeded to feed her just about anything: pizza and pancakes, cereal and potato chips, candy bars, Doritos, and anything that fell from the table. She grew. And she grew. And she grew some more, until she weighed almost a quarter of a ton. That's when her owners called the Funny Farm, begging us to take her in.

Poor Julie! At first, she was so rotund she could barely walk, and, if she tried, her belly would actually scrape the ground. Right away, we put her on a diet, and she didn't hide her displeasure. She pouted. She sulked. She turned up her snout at healthy grains and veggies. She seldom came out of her pig house, and ignored our overtures of friendship.

But gradually—very gradually, over the course of eighteen months or so—Julie came around. She shed 150 pounds and became much more active. She learned to prefer her new diet of hay, healthy pellets, and vegetables.

Best of all, she became very sweet and sociable, and now lives in our Pig Village, a line of new expanded pig condos designed to be warm and cozy in the winter and cool in the summer. Julie lives with another rescued mini-pig called Olive. It's interesting to note that Julie and Olive are the exact same breed and just about the same age, but Julie is at least twice Olive's size, even now that she's slimmed down. Be forewarned: that's what overfeeding can do to a "mini-pig."

Julie's favorite food is tomatoes, but because they're loaded with sugar, we save them as a special treat so our big girl will look good, feel great, and live a long, happy life.

7

The Facts of Life

O n the Funny Farm, the animals' upkeep was mostly the kids' job, right down to their shelter. Fortunately, the fields surrounding our house were full of old weather-beaten billboards, discarded lumber, broken pallets, junked plywood, and other raw materials. We would troop into the woods, collect what we needed, whip-tie it with a piece of rope, and haul it back in an old wheelbarrow or Flexible Flyer sled.

We got pretty good at slapping together lean-tos and sheds and coops. We covered them with wood slabs or tar paper and sided them with chicken wire. To the chicken houses, we added roosting perches and nesting boxes; we learned to do it right, and took pride in our handiwork. The enclosures sometimes listed crazily to one side, but they kept the animals safe and dry, and we didn't care about the aesthetics.

Sometimes we moaned about the dawn-to-dusk chores, but we knew that Mom couldn't do it all herself. Everybody pitched in to get things done, and we kids became very responsible at a very young age.

Being farm kids also gave us early lessons in the facts of life. I remember once seeing two dogs mating in a park, and a nearby parent explain to her child, "They were playing leapfrog and got stuck."

Mom was matter-of-fact about it. If one animal mounted another, she said, "They're mating. All animals mate. That's how it happens that there are always new animals when the old ones die off."

On the farm, somebody was always humping somebody else, or trying to. Seeing our stallion Shannon in an amorous state, pawing to get at a mare, a kid couldn't help but understand what went where and be very impressed.

Soon, barnyard sex didn't seem scandalous, or even particularly interesting. But the births that followed? Now, *they* never lost their thrill. I remember a spring day when one of our goats, heavily pregnant and wide as a barn, went into labor. On and off for twelve hours, I kept a vigil as she paced restlessly back and forth in her pen, as anxious as I was to get this show started. Aside from watching eggs hatch, this would be the first time I saw a birth up close.

The doe was still standing when her kid finally slid out, covered in a whitish goo that she immediately licked off. Within minutes, still damp from the womb, the baby struggled to its feet, tottered around the hay-strewn enclosure, then thrust its little nose into mom's underside and began to nurse.

It was messy. It was emotional. It was captivating.

The show wasn't over. This mama was a multitasker; as her first baby gulped down his first meal, she went on to deliver three more kids. Multiple births, twins and triplets, are common among goats, but quadruplets are very rare. That day, we got four for the price of one, and all the babies survived.

We saw sex. We saw birth. And we saw death.

I got firsthand experience in DIY butchery after three of our goats up and died from eating wild chokeberries. Curiously, chokeberries aren't toxic for people—we had often picked the dark purple, slightly sour fruits to make jam—but as we learned, to our sorrow, the seeds can be fatal to animals. And goats—well, they'll eat almost anything.

By then, several of our dearly departed pets were buried on the property, always sent off with a proper graveside service. When I heard about the goats, I went for the shovel, thinking, *Let's just get this over with.*

"Hold on a minute," Mom said, with that I've-got-a-brilliant-idea look. "The meat on those animals could feed us for months."

By then, I shouldn't have been surprised. After years of living in poverty—whatever the poverty level was back then, she must have walked it like a tightrope—Mom had begun to think like a survivalist. She threw nothing away, down to the tiniest scraps of paper. In our kitchen drawers were bundles of rubber bands, held together by other rubber bands, along with boxes of buttons, squares of aluminum foil that she used and reused, and safety pins of all sizes, pinned together like Christmas tree garland. She saved bags and paper clips and postage stamps that hadn't been canceled. As for clothes, she patched and mended ours until I wanted to scream—couldn't we for once get something new, with a price tag on it?

I understood her need to recycle. But our own goats?

I was repelled, but figured Mom would send the goats to the butcher, and the remains would come back in nicely wrapped brown paper packages for the freezer.

Not this time. She had found a book on livestock butchery—a sort of textbook, complete with illustrations, though thankfully, no photos. When I realized what she was thinking, I sputtered my protest, though by this time, I knew it was useless.

"Honey," Mom said, "I can't read the book and work at the same time. You have to help me."

So, working together, we learned how to butcher goats. Mom hung them from their heels on a tree branch, and I read aloud from the manual. It was a biology lesson like no other.

If only the faculty wives could have seen her that day: Anne Zaleski, once so delicate and demure, grunting and sweating as she gutted a bunch of goats. For months after that, she served goat stew, goat sausage, and goat jerky alongside our spaghetti. I continued to eat mayonnaise sandwiches.

It was a happy day when Mom finally got her driver's license, and we really celebrated the night she came home driving an old beater of a Mercury Comet, which once had been white but now was the color of week-old slush. Her first car! It wasn't much better than the broken-down jalopies on the trash heap next door—in fact, it probably belonged on the pile—but it was hers, and it ran. Usually.

Then one morning, heading out to Job No. 1, she discovered that the tires all had been flattened, slashed with an ice pick. That was the warning shot. From then on, the mischief that had plagued us when we'd first moved in was back, with a vengeance.

This time, the harassment took a more sinister turn. Unlike the teenagers who used to break into our house and steal our TVs or trash the living room, this perpetrator not only cut the tires but also severed the electric lines. The first time it happened, Mom put a good face on it, and even made it fun for us kids. "Okay, tonight we'll do our homework like they did in Ben Franklin's day—by candlelight!"

Reading in the half-gloom, as long shadows and candlelight flickered across the page, I would feel like Half-Pint in *Little House on the Prairie*. So, this was what it was like to be a pioneer girl! I didn't mind it a bit. Without electricity, everything in the fridge turned, goat meat included, but I didn't mind that, either, because that meant takeout food. Pizza!

But the vandalism didn't stop there. Next our water supply was cut off. In itself, this wasn't an uncommon occurrence; our water came from a well, and during cold spells the supply to our faucet sometimes slowed to a trickle. Whenever that happened, Mom ran a garden hose—multiple hoses, linked together—out the window, across the yard and down the gravel path to the outdoor spigot at the John Hancock office. But one frigid morning, when one of us turned on the faucet and nothing came out, Mom investigated. She discovered that the hose had been hacked to pieces.

She fixed it. It happened again. In fact, it happened so often, we were forced to collect water in a barrel in the kitchen, so we'd have enough to drink and wash with.

Out loud, we wondered if our teenage pranksters had made a comeback. But privately, each of us was thinking something else. These acts were more than destructive. They were sadistic. Cruel. *Personal.*

It crossed my mind that Dad might be behind these incidents, but I quickly pushed the idea away, as if I were forcing an intruder out the door. Dad may have been angry at Mom. He certainly was indifferent to our poverty. But surely, he was incapable of depriving his children of food and water and heat. Wasn't he?

The harassment didn't let up. After yet another tire-slashing incident, Mom slumped down on the back steps, put her head on her knees, and sobbed out loud. Replacing four tires would cost more than half her pay for that week.

She reported these incidents to the police, and each time they came out and made notes and filed reports. But our tormentor was good at his job. He slipped in and out unnoticed. With no evidence, the police could do nothing.

The enmity between my parents reached a new low one Sunday afternoon, after our usual weekend visiting Dad at Timber Heights Court.

As usual, we had changed from our nicely pressed play clothes to our rumpled farm gear and piled into his Cadillac, on our way back to the farm. As we drove out of the development, Dad nodded and waved like the pope to everyone on the circle.

I wasn't feeling a hundred percent—I had a mild fever, a ragged cough—and he wondered aloud if he should take me to see his doctor. Dad was a bit of a hypochondriac, and was always running to the doctor himself. And of course, he had retained custody of the pediatrician.

When we pulled up at the farmhouse, he leaned out the window and said to Mom, "Laurie has a fever. I think I'll keep her and take her to the doctor."

Mom peered in at me, then placed a hand on my forehead. She had never been much of a doctor-goer, and besides, weren't we farm folk now? Strong as horses. Just as healthy. She was like the patriarch in that movie, *My Big Fat Greek Wedding*—just spray some Windex on it, it'll be fine.

"She's got a runny nose," she said with a shrug. "If it gets worse, I'll take her to the doctor myself."

And just like that, their cool-but-civil conversation came to an abrupt end. Dad got that seething look, the one that always set my alarm bells clanging and caused the hairs on my neck and arms to raise up.

Trying to save the day, I piped up from the back seat, "I really don't feel so bad now, Dad! Thanks, Dad! See ya, Dad!" Then I grabbed my backpack and pushed open the car door.

"That's it," he said, and turned the key in the ignition. "Stay in the car, kids."

His words and tone made Mom flare. "Like hell they will! If Laurie needs a doctor, I will take her."

He started to pull away, and she began to pound on the car's hood, further enraging him.

"Don't you dare," she screamed. "Don't you dare take my children without my permission!"

Oh, Mom, I thought with despair. *Did you really have to dare him?*

"Kids, you just stay put!" he shouted.

The car lurched forward, I toppled back against the seat, and we were off, in a swirling cloud of dust.

Cathy turned and glared at me stonily: *Look what you've done.* Stephen was fretful. We were jostling down the dirt path back to the highway when suddenly there was a great thumping sound behind us. I turned to look out the back window, and gasped— Mom had taken a flying leap, landed on the trunk of the car, and was holding on with both hands, swearing a blue streak.

Instead of slowing down, Dad hit the accelerator, barreled down that bumpy dirt road, then turned a hard left onto the highway. All the way back to his house, as Mom clung to the back of the car, he deliberately zigzagged back and forth across the yellow line, trying to shake her off. It was a nightmare. In the back seat, all three of us kids were hysterically crying and pleading for him to stop.

In traffic, cars and trucks blared their horns. I saw the faces of drivers, shocked to see a woman clinging to the trunk of a speeding Cadillac. I looked back at Mom, who was clearly terrified but unable to let go. Any second, I expected her to fly off into a ditch or under the wheels of a semitruck. I glimpsed my dad's eyes in the rearview mirror. He wore the same glacial look he'd had the night he held us at knifepoint in Cathy's bedroom.

At last he pulled into Timber Heights Court. The neighbors— many of them were out gardening or barbecuing on a Sunday— watched openmouthed as the Caddy flew into the cul-de-sac with a hysterical woman gripping the back like a misplaced hood ornament. He screeched into our driveway and hit the brake, and Mom slid off onto the concrete.

Someone along the way must have called the police, because

almost immediately, a trio of squad cars pulled in behind us. The aftermath was a blur of cops and flashing lights. My father stood there, arms across his chest, still belligerent. My mother shouted and cried. Her fingernails were torn, her fingertips bloody. I remember being simultaneously relieved that Mom was alive after that wild ride, but mortified that all this was happening in full view of the neighbors. They certainly were getting a different look at my father and our family.

And so, the battling Zaleskis were hauled back into family court. Cathy, Stephen, and I stood before yet another disgusted judge and described the incident as we had witnessed it.

I never did know what Dad's punishment was, but it must have been insignificant to the point of being meaningless. Despite what he'd done, we were still required to visit him on a weekly basis, but from that time on our parents had to hand us off at the police station. It wasn't polite. It wasn't pretty. But they didn't dare step out of line. Not with the cops watching.

Animal Tails

Stinky the Skunk

It's not a very original name, is it? And in this case, it's not at all accurate. Born and raised in captivity, our "Stinky" was neutered and descented by his first owner, an exotic animal breeder, and then sold to a young couple who intended to keep him as a pet. The plan might have worked out if they'd had a proper skunk house, separate from their own living quarters. But they lived in a condominium. Not an ideal setup.

I've had several skunks over the years, and I couldn't love these animals more. They're bright and friendly. They can be litter-trained, just like cats. There's just one drawback, and it's a biggie.

Skunks are nocturnal. They sleep most of the day, then forage, eat, and play at night. Some people insist skunks can adjust to a day-time schedule, but none of mine ever have.

As you can imagine, it didn't take long for the couple to tire of Stinky's all-night carousing. He stopped using his litter box and dug holes in the carpet. Soon, the woman issued an ultimatum: either the skunk had to go, or her husband would. Reluctantly, he brought his pet to the Funny Farm.

I didn't have a proper skunk shelter or even a decent animal crate, so for the first few weeks Stinky lived inside the farmhouse, roaming free. Talk about sleepless nights. He had an unerring internal clock that seemed to wake him just as I was drifting off. And that's when the party started. All night long, I could hear him opening and shutting the kitchen cabinets, nosing around for scraps of food, and pulling apart trash bags. His favorite pastime was tearing into the Tupperware. By morning, the kitchen would be an obstacle course of overturned plastic containers. It was time to move Stinky outside.

Without the scent glands that allow skunks to spray, domesticated skunks are basically "unarmed," almost defenseless against predators, even though they have a nice set of long, curved claws. So Stinky's shelter had to be big enough so that he could play, burrow, and enjoy the outdoors, but also be completely secure. A nice family built him a large wooden enclosure with an indoor house and lots of room outside, all enclosed with chicken wire.

Shortly after Stinky moved into his new home, his former owner returned, saying he missed Stinky and wanted to take him back.

"Stop right there," I said, "and explain to me how your situation is any different. Do you have a different home? A different place for Stinky to live? A different wife?"

The answers were no, no, and no. Stinky stayed at the farm, where he continues his nocturnal ways. He's a digger, and he's been known to tunnel underground from his house to the nearby souvenir shop, where he steals stuffed animals and takes them to his quarters.

Though skunks are solitary animals, Stinky enjoys company, and each visiting day, all I have to do is call his name for him to yawn and stretch and emerge from his burrow to meet our visitors. Kids especially love meeting him and getting a selfie with Stinky, our famous skunk.

8

Jersey Devils

I was a good student and really enjoyed school, despite the social hierarchy that separated me from my peers. I had only to look at most of my classmates, especially the girls in their fashionable gear from Casual Corner and the Deb Shoppe, to feel like second-hand Rose in my threadbare clothes.

On the farm I was a tomboy, an ass-kicker, Tarzan and Jane rolled up into one propulsive locomotive of a girl. Sometimes in school, I felt like somebody pulled the plug. I was self-conscious and awkward, all elbows and knobby knees and ladder legs. Between classes I walked those long hallways with hunched shoulders, turtling into myself, eyes fixed on the floor tiles as if they were the most fascinating things on earth. I prayed I wouldn't attract attention, but I was hard to miss. Well on my way to my adult height of five feet ten inches, I towered over the other kids, including the boys.

At recess, I was called names like "Beanpole" and "Giraffe." One smartass made points with his pals when he referred to me as "Amazon girl." Worst of all was the time someone called me the Jolly Green Giant—it was a boy I secretly liked.

I went home crying to Mom, who looked me up and down, and in a serious tone said, "Well, what do you think about us cutting off your feet? Then you'd be shorter. Maybe we could cut you off at the knees."

I did a snort-laugh through my tears.

"Come on, honey," she said. She took my face in her hands and looked deep into my eyes. "Someday, you're going to love being just the way you are, tall and beautiful, standing out in a crowd, head and shoulders above all the rest. Until then, have a good cry, because, as you know . . ."

"I know," I said, and wiped my nose on my sleeve. "The more I cry, the less I pee."

"Exactly."

"Besides, you're strong enough to whup all those kids, including the boys."

And I was.

One day at recess, I overheard a kid on the schoolyard use the word "Piney," and instantly, others took up the chant: "Piney! Piney!"

I had no idea what it meant, but from their jeering tone, I knew it was an insult at the very least, and maybe even a dirty word. I swept the schoolyard with my eyes, hopeful they were taunting someone else, not me.

In time, I learned that "Piney" was a slur used against people who lived in the New Jersey Pinelands, also called the Pine Barrens. Supposedly, Pineys were goobers, rubes, *Deliverance* types who married their cousins and lived with their pigs and played a really mean banjo.

By far the most famous resident of the Pine Barrens was a mythical beast called the Jersey Devil, the malformed thirteenth child of a backwoods woman called Mother Leeds. According to local lore, he had horns and hooves, wings like a bat and a forked tail like Satan. He supposedly flew around the pine forests killing livestock and pets and going up and down chimneys, sort of like the anti-Claus. In the early nineteenth century, some "witnesses" claimed he looked like a big flying kangaroo, others said an ostrich, and some a possum. So much for eyewitness testimony.

Geographically speaking, I was not a Piney, because the Funny Farm was located on the outskirts of the Pinelands. But that was cold comfort. We had a pig and a goose in the house. A horse had just moved out. We fit the description. That's when I made a vow: no one must ever know where or how I lived.

Every day, when the school bus dropped me near the John Hancock office, I would run like a streak down that dirt road, praying no one would see our rundown house, stuck in a field next to Mount Trashmore, surrounded by pigs, goats, and hens.

I should mention that nowadays, the people once denigrated as Pineys have claimed the name as a badge of honor. Around South Jersey, it's not uncommon to see bumper stickers that say "Piney Power." But back then, it was a putdown, an insult—shorthand for anyone who was rural and poor.

I know how my mother felt about it. We weren't Pineys, but what if we had been? Did any of the other kids at school know how to build a lean-to shelter from scrap wood or ride a horse bareback or give a pig a mani-pedi or play midwife to a pregnant goat? We should be proud of who we were. For all of our deprivations, all of us were honor students, at the top of our class. So much for goobers and rubes.

But early on, it made me wonder: Why do people always find reasons to look down on one another?

I was one of a handful of "underprivileged children" who happened to live inside the bounds of a well-to-do school district.

It was a special trial for me to line up for free school lunches, which we got in exchange for a special ticket. Each day, I'd hide my ticket in my palm and pass it surreptitiously to the lunch lady, like a spy handing off a secret message. Then I'd grab my tray and race to my seat in the cafeteria, cheeks burning with shame.

For the first time, I began to feel angry about my poverty. It made me furious when we ran out of bread, or when Mom bought the cheap mayo, or when I couldn't afford to buy a used book at the school book fair. I also started to want things other kids had—Jordache and Sergio Valente jeans, Nike sneakers—and feel upset that I couldn't have them.

Our poverty was exposed in other ways. For several years, we didn't have a telephone at the farm. As much as we kids begged, according to Mom, it was just another bill she couldn't afford to pay. Whenever she had to fill out a school form, like permission for a field trip, she'd write "N/A" in that space. "Not applicable." Some of my teachers actually got annoyed at me for turning in incomplete forms, and in one instance, one of them waved me to the front of the class to ask for my phone number.

Keeping my back to my classmates, I mumbled that we had no phone.

"I'm sorry?" she said, leaning forward. "Please speak up, Laurie."

I dipped my head and said, "We don't have a telephone." Then I raised my eyes and looked at her pleadingly.

Please don't make me say it again.

Her eyebrows lifted, then comprehension flooded her face, and she laid her hand on mine. "Laurie, thank you for explaining. It's fine."

I hurried back to my desk, hoping against hope that my classmates hadn't heard the exchange. After that, my teacher treated me with a tenderness that felt good but also made me ache inside. She felt sorry for me, and like charity, like being called underprivileged, it was almost more than I could bear. Sometimes I gave the Timber Heights Court number as my own, and Dad's address, too, though it made me feel slightly disloyal to Mom.

I was over the moon the day when we got a phone. But that abbreviation—N/A—has the power to change my frame of mind, even today. Just seeing it, in passing, on a piece of paper, takes me right back to that day, to the front of the class, when my biggest worry in life was that the other kids would discover that I was poor. Those two letters felt like a personal defect, or failing: I was N/A. N/A. N/A.

Of us all, I think Stephen was hurt the most by our folks' breakup. Because he was so young—barely four when we first moved away from Timber Heights—he'd had fewer experiences with the violence at home and he picked up on the stigma of being a boy without a dad. Back then, hardly any of the kids we knew had parents who were separated or divorced. It's hard to believe now, but at the time, such things were still spoken about in whispers.

I had hoped against hope that, when the dust settled, my parents would learn to be friends. I had heard of such miracles, grown-ups acting like grown-ups and going from being husband and wife to being cooperative co-parents. How nice that would have been— how wonderfully calm and safe. It didn't happen.

To our embarrassment, Dad made no attempt to hide his girlfriends, a chorus line of fresh-faced college students, mostly blondes, all infatuated with the brilliant Professor Zaleski. In their company, his swagger increased, as did his chest circumference. Stephen remembers a few of the girls trying to get on his good side, even acting motherly toward him, though they were scarcely out of their teens. Then they'd play with him, like the kids they still were.

They tried to be nice to me, too, but I had a mother, thank you, and I said so—in other words, "Get lost." And heaven help the girl who tried to ingratiate herself with Cathy. My sister made it crystal clear how she felt: the girls were pathetic, and our dad was the most pathetic of all.

But he got away with everything, it seemed, with few repercussions, including kidnapping. It started when we went for a weekend to his house at the Jersey Shore. Two days stretched into four, then a week, then two, and still he made no noises about taking us home, though we'd only packed enough clothes for a weekend.

Perplexed, we asked if we could call our mom, but he refused. Finally, Cathy and I slipped away from the beach house, and walked several blocks downtown to a phone booth. Mom answered on the first ring, breathlessly, and when she heard our voices, began to cry. "Girls, Jesus God, where have you been? Did the police come? Is Stephen all right?"

Dad had breached the custody agreement by keeping us without informing our mother, and though she went to the police, they took no action. She didn't have a car at the time—she was riding her horse to work—and couldn't look for us herself.

At dinnertime, a police cruiser pulled up in front of the Wildwood beach house, its red lights spinning, and two officers ordered Dad to turn us over, or else. We grabbed our bags, were hustled into the back seat, and the police drove us home.

My only explanation is that, at that time, the concept of parental abduction didn't exist, or wasn't strictly enforced. Dad had kidnapped us, and when Mom went to the police, there was nothing they could or were willing to do.

After we moved away from Timber Heights Court, I noticed that Mom became much less receptive to hugs and kisses. It's no wonder. She was a harried single parent with three kids, three jobs, a dozen animals, and a gazillion responsibilities. The lack of privacy didn't help, and she could be touchy and irritable by the end of the day.

But I never doubted her love for me and my siblings, and never felt it more than the day she bought me a new toy—one she couldn't afford, which I didn't need, and which I already had at my father's house. I remember the jubilation I felt when I came home from school one afternoon to find it on my bed—brand-new, price tag and all.

"A Barbie head!"

I hung on my mother like wallpaper, so hard she had to forcibly peel me off.

"Okay, Laurie," she said, and headed out of the room. "I'm glad you like it."

"Thank you, Mom!" I called after her, and danced around the room with the head cradled in my arms.

Then I got out my art supplies, found a black Sharpie pen, and wrote in block letters on the bottom: "Property of Laurie Zaleski."

I did the same with everything—clothes, schoolbooks, shoes—to prove I owned something in this world. It didn't always work, though. Once at a skating rink, I left my favorite green hoodie on the bleachers and someone walked off with it, despite my name emblazoned, big as life, on the inside collar.

It was my one item of clothing that Mom had saved for and bought new, and I wore it over everything. She would not be able to replace it. I grieved the loss for weeks.

One magical day, my social status in school changed in a blink, and for the better. Mom had the outrageous idea to come to show-and-tell with the young black Angus steer we were raising, called Harry Hamburger.

At first, I was aghast. Did she want to ruin me, and make sure that I was never accepted by my classmates? Did she want everyone to know we were Pineys?

But it turned out to be the greatest day ever. Kids and teachers by the dozens spilled out of their classroom doors to gape at Mom walking down the hall, with Harry placidly clopping along on a lead beside her, and the principal scurrying behind, cleaning up a trail of cow manure.

In homeroom, my classmates lined up to pet Harry and feed him snacks as Mom told them about animal care and farm life. Harry loved the attention, and delighted everyone when he let out a big, soulful *mooooooo*. The commotion was so great, other teachers let their students crowd in, too, until it was wall-to-wall kids, all of them thrilled to see a cow at the head of the class.

We were the talk of the school, instant celebrities—Mom, Harry, and me. In the days that followed, kids who hadn't taken much notice of me before came sidling up in the hall or at recess, filled with questions about the farm and our other animals. "You have chickens and pigs, too? Your goat's having babies? Wow. Awesome."

Thinking back, I probably felt a lot like Sally Field, when she won her second Academy Award. "You like me! You really like me!"

Basking in my newfound fame, I realized that all the time I'd spent longing to be one of the rich kids, deep down, at least a couple of those rich kids would have loved to live on a farm. It was a life-changing discovery, for all the Zaleski kids. Suddenly, it was not just okay to be us, but cool and even enviable. Weird in the best way. Our homesteading, sod-busting lifestyle wasn't pitiful, but marvelously fun and offbeat.

Kids started coming over to ride horses, climb trees, and get into all kinds of mischief and dirt. We built campfires and made s'mores and slept under the stars. When we joined Scouts, Mom was the most popular den mother, hands down, and all our friends clamored to be in her troop. Later on, when Cathy and I joined the school band, Mom was driving a thirdhand electric company van with a stick on the column that became the bandwagon. It was camo green and had no seats, but no worries. The band members would pile aboard and sit on folding chairs or bales of hay or on the floor. Everybody thought it was a hoot.

Not to say I didn't still feel twinges of envy to see other kids in their nice clothes, living in their nice homes, with two nice, loving parents under one roof. But there was currency in our way of living, too. I started to take pride in who I was. I started to understand that, while I didn't choose this life, it worked, in an unorthodox way, against all the odds.

Though Mom was known as the fun mom, she was strict when it counted, especially when it came to learning. In our house, you buckled down or else. And as early as elementary school, Mom warned, "I can't afford to send you to college, so you'll all have to get scholarships. Now crack those books."

Cathy was the best reader of the family, so smart, always in advanced classes and topping the honor roll. For her, learning was like falling off a log. Stephen was brilliant at math and economics, like Dad, and from the time he was a boy—I'm talking seven and eight years old—he'd send for trial subscriptions of *Forbes* and *Barron's*, and read them with as much interest as Spider-Man comics.

Although I, too, was in advanced classes and always made the honor roll, I had to work twice as hard to get good grades. I had college on my mind all through school. My niche was art. I imagined a fabulous career as a painter, a fashion designer, a Disney animator, or an art teacher. Mom called me "poky Laurie" and "flaky Laurie," the one with my head in the clouds, but she supported me a thousandfold. Her belief in her children was like an article of faith.

Dad, on the other hand, dismissed my ambition as idle dreaming, saying there was no money in art. "What do you want to do," he asked, "end up in the poorhouse?"

Even as a young girl, I recognized the irony of his statement, and dared myself to say what I was thinking: "Dad, I've lived in the poorhouse most of my life, and so have my sister and brother. You put us there, remember?"

Even if there was no money in art, there was *art* in art. I couldn't envision my life without it.

I suppose it says something about me that the artist I admired most was Norman Rockwell, and he's still one of my favorites. I was transfixed by his *Saturday Evening Post* covers, with their near-photographic realism, and charmed by his idyllic view of American life: boys and girls flirting at the soda fountain, families gathered for Thanksgiving, kids running from a swimming hole. I liked the famous painting of Rockwell drawing Rockwell. I admired his stirring illustrations of the civil rights era. I adored his depiction of a disheveled girl sitting outside the principal's office, smirking, with a black eye—clearly, she had just won a fistfight, presumably with a boy. I identified with that girl. She was a scrapper.

I wanted life to be like one of those Norman Rockwell paintings—full of humor and hope and happy endings.

Lots and lots of happy endings.

It was about that time I started saying to Mom, "Just you wait. Someday, when I'm a famous artist, I'm going to buy you a real farm, and you can have all the animals you want."

"Okay," said Mom. "I'll mark someday on my calendar."

Little did I know that those words—that idle dreaming—would direct most of the rest of my life. Over the years, I would repeat the promise, like an incantation.

My happiness in school was quenched the day I came home to find that Harry Hamburger was gone.

The clue, of course, was in his name. Turns out Mom had

agreed to raise Harry for a neighborhood merchant in exchange for a side of beef after he was slaughtered. We're talking hundreds of pounds of meat, enough to feed our family (with one abstention) for at least a year, maybe more. Between Harry and the occasional chicken, we were set, and our grocery bills were slashed to the price of spaghetti and a few staples.

I had loved Harry, who was big as a moose, gentle as a kitten, and tame as any of our dogs. He always loved a good butt rub, a kiss on the nose, and a big fistful of fresh, sweet hay. I had been especially grateful to him for his star turn in the classroom, which changed the way kids treated me in school.

Mom heard out my tearful tirade, then said gently, "Laurie, he was never ours to keep. I'm sorry. This is the bargain I made, and this is what I had to do. We need to eat."

But I was inconsolable, and kept a framed photo of Harry on a shelf in the living room, like a shrine. For a very long time, whenever Mom served burgers, steak, or meatballs, I would leave the table in tears and stand in the kitchen, snuffling loudly, as I spread up another mayonnaise sandwich.

Soon after that our financial situation improved appreciably because of a man who would become like a second father to us—and by second father, I mean as unpredictable and unreliable as the first.

Animal Tails

Cowboy

For several days running, a South Jersey girl and her mother heard high-pitched, anguished cries coming from the farm next door. When they investigated, they discovered that a newborn goat kid, confined in too-close quarters with a horse, had been repeatedly kicked, and now had broken bones. They approached the pen and watched as the kid struggled to stand, bleating pathetically.

Mom and daughter searched out the farm owner and demanded to know why he didn't get help. His reply was right to the point: "Not that it's any of your damned business, but it's a dumb animal, a damned goat. And I can't afford any more damned vet bills."

Clearly, like some people, this man was of the opinion that "dumb" animals feel no pain, or maybe their pain doesn't hurt as much as people's pain. Hey, he was just being honest. He really didn't give a damn.

At that point, it would have been easier for the mom and daughter to walk away. After all, the goat was the farmer's legal property. Who were they to interfere? I'm glad to say they laid down the law, and said he had two choices: turn over the little goat or answer to animal welfare authorities.

The farmer didn't put up a fight—this was his chance to get rid of a problem—and that's how the goat came to the Funny Farm. From here, we rushed him to the New Bolton Center, where vets warned that surgery to mend his fractured front leg could cost more than three thousand dollars and would require pins.

I have a standard reply in cases like this: "Well, that's what credit cards are for."

The story of the injured goat is especially wonderful for me, because it brought home in a powerful way how many people support what we do. I was especially proud of the mom and daughter who saved him and stood up for what was right. Our social media volunteer had an idea to post the story on Facebook, speaking in the goat's voice. I didn't love the idea, and said, "My animals don't dress up and they don't talk." He convinced me to try it, and in a matter of hours donations started flooding in. We received enough to cover the surgery and then some, all with love notes and get-well messages for the goat I named Cowboy, due to his black-and-white fur and bowed legs. This was the first time I didn't have to use my own money to pay a vet bill.

Cowboy is a LaMancha goat, a breed supposedly descended from Spanish dairy goats. LaManchas stand out because of their tiny "gopher ears" and their unabashed love of people and food. If you visit the Funny Farm today, you can't miss the healthy, strong, and strapping Cowboy, who's known among our volunteers and visitors as the "Donations Inspector." Cowboy inspects all of the donations to be sure they're good for the others. If you don't watch out, he'll climb into your car in search of Cheerios, Goldfish crackers, and other tasty treats. He's the first Funny Farm animal who spoke on social media, and the world fell in love with him.

PART II

Annie's Girl

9

Father Figure

I f you don't start flying this plane, start saying your prayers, because we're going down. And fast."

The two-seat Cessna trainer, not much bigger than a Volkswagen, yawed on a current of air high above the South Jersey countryside. From the right-hand window, I gaped down at a jigsaw pattern of farms, fields, and Matchbox cars crawling along the roads and highways.

As I cowered in the passenger seat, the pilot released the yoke, leaned back, and popped the top on a Budweiser can, slurping at the foam that flowed over the side. Casually, in no hurry at all as the plane pitched and bucked, he pulled a pack of Winstons from his shirt pocket, shook out a smoke, and fished in the same pocket for a light.

I must have looked like Edvard Munch's *The Scream*—openmouthed and mute with terror. Unperturbed, he glanced over at me as if we were passing the time over tea, not teetering in an unmanned aircraft, three thousand feet up.

"In the next ten seconds," he said coolly, "you will fly this plane."

That's when *The Scream* came to life.

"Barney, I can't! I don't know how!"

"Start by taking the controls."

He glanced at his wristwatch.

"You've got eight seconds. Seven. Six . . ."

His name was John Gordon Oldfield Jr., but everybody called him Barney, after Barney Oldfield, a famous race car driver of the early 1900s. Mom first met him on the Wildwood boardwalk, where he made and sold blown-glass figurines: clowns, Christmas trees, carousels with tiny horses—tiny works of art, all very colorful, iridescent, and delicate. Both Mom and Barney were lonesome and disappointed by love, so they tied their lives together like rafts adrift at sea, and towed the kids along in their wake.

Barney was an Air Force veteran who had repaired aircraft at a base on Okinawa during the Vietnam War. He was extraordinarily bright and well-read, the kind of guy who knew something about everything. History. Geography. Religion. Politics. He would have killed on *Jeopardy!*

Glass-blowing was Barney's art, hobby, and side hustle; from nine to five, he was an auto mechanic who also raced and restored classic cars, including the all-time coolest-ever sports car: a 1960 Austin-Healey Bugeye Sprite.

I suppose I could understand my mother's attraction to this broad-shouldered, roughly handsome guy, with his moustache, long, limp ponytail, John Lennon glasses, and *Easy Rider* attitude. Barney had the kind of personality that can be irresistible to some women: overwhelming maleness combined with deep sensitivity. It was his arms and hands I noticed first—they were big, bronze, and powerful-looking. Like Alley Oop's.

He and his son Gordon lived in Audubon, a small town about a half hour up the Atlantic City Expressway. When he and Mom became a couple, we sometimes spent nights up there. I remember sleeping—or trying to sleep—in a room directly over his basement workshop, where he toiled into the wee hours, making those blown-glass clowns and carousels, using a Pyrex torch clamped to his worktable, a converted steel door. To this day, I can smell the molten glass and cigarette smoke and hear the muffled rock music reverberating through the floorboards, all night long. Led Zeppelin. Aerosmith. The Beatles.

It was a far cry from the old days, when I used to listen in on Dad and Mom having their fancy cocktail parties, with the trays of hors d'oeuvres and martinis and Jell-O molds. Now it was beer and Jack Daniel's instead of cocktails, and instead of Mom playing show tunes on the grand piano, it was Barney thumping out rock music on the stereo. I remember how the floor would shake when Elton John sang, "B-B-B-Bennie and the Jets. . . ."

Back and forth our two families went, from Audubon to Turnersville, from Turnersville to Audubon, until Barney and Gordon, then five years old, decided to move to the Funny Farm. I hear you: If Mom and Barney wanted to be together, why didn't we move to his place, a three-bedroom suburban house, where we could live like semi-normal people?

I think Mom was gun-shy, and, after Dad, who could blame her? She wasn't willing to throw in her lot with any man, at least not in any permanent way. If she didn't uproot us from our schools when she left Dad, she sure wasn't going to do it for Barney.

And besides, she asked, "If we move, who's going to take care of the animals?"

The upshot was, Barney sold his place, and he and Gordon crowded in with us. If four people in a one-bedroom house was a tight squeeze, six people was a sardine tin. And six people plus a couple dozen animals was a rodeo.

Even then, our family continued to grow. Mom had an open-door policy, and over the years let in many homeless, rootless, love-less people who, like the rescue animals, became part of our family, if only for a time. Like Jimmy Bacon, a local boy whose mother had died of cancer, and then tragically lost his dad and brother in a house fire. Darling Jimmy came to us at the age of seventeen, a wounded bird, confused and grief-stricken, but sweet and kind. He was the best kind of big brother.

In exchange for a place to hang his hat—he preferred to live out of a car on our lot so he'd have an inkling of privacy—Jimmy was our go-to babysitter and became a lifelong friend. At a time when homosexuality was still considered scandalous, when coming out could be frightening or even dangerous, Mom helped Jimmy come to grips with being gay and not see himself as flawed in any way. The whole love-is-love thing—Mom came to that conclusion a lot sooner than many people.

Then there was a woman we called Aunt Beanie who, like Mom, had been left destitute and homeless when she divorced her husband. Once quite a wealthy woman, Beanie slept for months in a bedroll on our living room floor and when she left, gave us some of her beautiful clothing. For almost a year, we also made room for a foster child named Steven. Mom loved and protected Steven until a more suitable home was found for him.

At night, when everybody headed for bed—whether it was an actual bed or just a spot on the floor—it was like *The Waltons*.

Good night, Beanie.

Good night, Jimmy.

Good night, John-Boy.

Our half-a-house turned into a halfway house for runaways and ragamuffins of all kinds, including school friends who, for what-ever reason, fell out with their parents. They all confided in my mother, who dispensed advice like PEZ candies and had more aphorisms than Dear Abby.

As always, her motto, "The more you cry, the less you'll pee," always got a laugh, and seemed to dispel the blues, at least a little bit.

In many ways, Mom's new boyfriend Barney enriched our lives. He drove us kids to study harder and learn more. He provided a level of economic stability we hadn't known in years. And he gave us a second brother in Gordon, whom we picked on at first, but ultimately grew to love (and, come to think of it, continued to pick on).

Barney settled the turf war in the girls' bedroom, building a bunk bed so Cathy and I no longer had to sleep side by side. Then he built a second bunk bed, because we couldn't decide who should get to sleep on top.

He taught Stephen to scuba dive. He taught me to fix cars. He showed shutterbug Mom how to take better pictures. She was totally snap-happy and a day never passed without her pulling out her ever-present Kodak Sun, but Barney was a real photographer, with a 35-millimeter SLR and all the bulky equipment. His specialty was landscapes, and he developed his photos in our darkened bathroom. I hung over his shoulder as he worked, and took mental notes that would come in handy years later, when I became a professional photographer.

Barney also made much better use of the land surrounding our house. He got a rototiller and planted long rows of rotating crops: corn, tomatoes, lettuce, and watermelon in the summer, carrots, onions, parsnips, and spinach in the fall. The kids made up the weed patrol. We weeded until our hands were raw and our backs half-broken. While we detested the labor, we felt amazed and proud when real edible things started to come out of the earth we had so carefully tended. From that time on, we had fresh vegetables almost year-round, enough for the family, and enough to spare for the animals.

I have mixed feelings about Barney and about my mother's long devotion to him. But I'll always be grateful to him for one thing. He taught me to fly—me, the scaredy-cat who wouldn't even ride the Ferris wheel.

It all started on his birthday, when Mom gave him a few lessons out of Cross Keys Airport in Williamstown.

Well, Barney took to the air like Lindbergh. He went on to get his pilot's license, then started taking us all up, one at a time, for Sunday-afternoon joyrides. For some reason, he decided I should try my hand at flying, too. According to him, of all four kids, I was the one with the interest and the aptitude.

I wasn't sure I agreed, especially at three thousand feet, when he took those big hands off the controls and ordered me to take over. I'd do it, sure, but not because I wanted to fly. I just didn't want to die. Sometimes during those flights, Barney would force the Cessna into hair-raising maneuvers, pulling the yoke into his chest to propel it into a near-vertical climb. At that point the plane would stall out, nosedive, and spiral down in a tight spin. All pilots practice stalls in case of emergency, but they don't do it like Barney. He seemed to enjoy terrifying me, while remaining unnaturally composed himself. He must have had nerves of steel. Or maybe it was the beer.

When we fell out of a stall, it felt like we were circling the drain; in the dead silence before the engine sputtered back to life, I could just about get through one Hail Mary. Returning to the airport, we would fly perilously low, buzzing the treetops and picking up leaves in our landing gear.

Every week, in tears, I would swear to Mom that I was never, ever going up again. But the next weekend, when Barney said,

"Come on kids, we're all going to the airport," I always went, and always found myself up there in the copilot's seat, saying my Hail Marys.

If word had spread about Barney's unorthodox teaching methods—smoking and drinking in flight, especially with a kid in the next seat—he would have been grounded for sure. And though I disagree with stark terror and fear of death as motivators, they did get the job done. In spite of my genuine fear, I had never felt so unquenchably alive. Soon I couldn't tell the difference between fear and exhilaration. I can't express how proud I felt when I overheard Barney say to Mom, "Anne, she's got a real feel for it. She's eleven years old, and, darn it, the kid can fly."

Because of him, I'm a pilot today.

Unfortunately, on land and in the air, Barney was a drinking man. Starting with an eye-opener in the morning—a shot and a beer, and even pouring beer into his eggs—he picked up again at happy hour, and that hour continued until all hours. Barney wasn't a happy drunk. Alcohol rubbed his nerves raw. It made him short-tempered, irritable, and far less willing to put up with the antics of four boisterous kids.

His drinking worsened over time, until he could toss back a pint of Jack Daniel's before noon and still function. Occasionally he would reach the limits of his tolerance, and in an instant go from an upright lucid adult to a stumblebum, slurring his words and shambling unsteadily.

Barney was reckless in many ways. As you can probably guess from his daredevil piloting, he was an aggressive driver, too. At the time, New Jersey had a lot more traffic circles, or roundabouts. Drivers seem to approach these intersections in one of two ways:

as a terrifying death spiral or a challenging game of bumper cars. Barney was in the second category. He took those circles at such high speeds—steering with his pinky finger!—that the wheels on one side of the car would lift clear off the ground. At those times, even my mother, a legendary lead-foot, would clutch his arm and whisper, "A little slower, Barn, please. A little slower."

He was also a disciplinarian of the old school—as in the Roman coliseum school. If one of the kids did something wrong, he would force the offender to stand in the backyard and hold up bricks as a form of punishment. It was torture. I remember how it felt to hold those bricks straight out at my sides for a half hour or more, until they felt as heavy as boulders. If my arms dropped, Barney would holler, "Get 'em up!" All of us had our turn. We had no choice but to comply with these punishments, sniveling like babies.

Similarly, when Barney caught Stephen and Gordon fighting— not an uncommon occurrence between brothers—he wouldn't break it up, but make them fight more, like gladiators. "You wanna fight? Okay, then, let's really fight!" And as he looked on, they would beat the piss out of each other, bawling all the while.

One time, when he caught Stephen peeing on Gordon's ankle, Barney made both boys strip down in the backyard and have a pee-off, urinating all over each other. The last squirt to squirt was the winner. You've got to give him points for originality.

While these punishments may have been cruel, they weren't necessarily unusual for the time. Many parents and even teachers believed in and practiced corporal punishment—the whole spare-the-rod school of thought. And to the Zaleski kids, having seen and experienced much worse at our father's house, these forms of discipline seemed almost tame by comparison.

Even so, we complained repeatedly to our mother, enough so

that she and Barney had it out. While the punishments didn't end, they were fewer and certainly less imaginative.

Suffice it to say that Mom didn't quite lose her "stand-by-your-man" attitude when she left Dad. She stood by Barney and defended him, even to us, her children. I can't explain it except to say she was a product of her times. She broke with convention in so many ways. She raised herself up as she raised us up. But there's no getting around it. She had impeccably bad taste in men, and she tended to defer to them. With Barney, she was two for two.

Not surprisingly, Dad and Barney loathed each other. Sometimes Barney would accompany Mom to the police station to drop us off for our weekend visits. My dad would give Barney his best laser stare and mutter, "You stinking pothead. You loser. You derelict." If looks could kill, Barney would have been instantly vaporized. I have to hand it to him that he never responded in kind, never retaliated, and barely raised an eyebrow in the face of the barrage of insults.

His indifference must have driven Dad crazy—or crazier.

===== **Animal Tails** =====

Adele
"So a chicken walks into a chiropractor's . . ."

It sounds like the setup for a joke, but it's just another day in the life of the Funny Farm.

One of our best-known residents is a pampered Buff Orpington hen with a redhead's temper and attitude. From the day I got Adele—she was surrendered to the farm with a half-dozen other homeless chickens—she was the only one who refused to live among the hundreds of other birds on the grounds. It was as if for her, this commoners' existence was simply out of the question. Every time I put Adele out in the farmyard, she would circle around to the back deck, stand at the sliding glass door, and peck relentlessly until I let her in again. It was clear that Adele was determined to be my new roommate. She never gave up. How could I say no? She finally won and loved living with the dogs and cats in the house. She loves to jump up on the couch and watch TV—her favorite show is *Friends*—clucking the whole time!

You cannot potty-train a chicken. Believe me, I tried. So I outfitted Adele with a diaper—essential for the house-dwelling hen—and then built a cardboard house with a special roost for her to sleep in. She was the happiest hen ever. Whenever I couldn't find her, she was always in the bathroom playing in my jewelry, with some of the necklaces hanging around her neck. Adele loved anything sparkly, and would stare into the mirror for hours and hours. Anytime I took the dogs on road trips, Adele would come along too, claiming the center armrest of the truck to get the best view. Adele ruled the roost and none of the dogs or cats ever stood up to her.

One day, I left the house for a chiropractic adjustment and, unbeknownst to me, Adele decided to tag along. Somehow, she slipped out behind me, jumped up into the truck bed, and off I went. When I was finished with my appointment, I heard all this talk of rooster, chicken, rooster, chicken. As I approached the receptionist, I noticed she was holding a chicken. I asked how she got a chicken and she said it came up and knocked on the door. I said, "She looks a lot like my house chicken, Adele, what are you going to do with her?" The receptionist said she had a small farm and was going to take her home and build her a pen *outside*! I said, "Okay, if you need any help, let me know, I own the Funny Farm."

For two days, I searched high and low for Adele, all over the farm. Finally, one morning over coffee, the bells in my head went off and I realized that Adele must have jumped into the back of my truck.

I felt like a terrible mom! I called the receptionist and told her that was my Adele! She laughed and said I could come pick her up. I rushed to her house to find Adele pacing back and forth in a nice outside pen! She was very put out!

She squawked at me all the way home. When we got home, I painted her nails to be sure I would always recognize her. After I told the social media volunteer the story, he wrote the story from Adele's point of view and posted it on Facebook. To date, it has been one of our most-viewed posts, and certainly the most talked about. He wrote, "I was just laying in the back of the truck and it started to move. I went faster and faster until it was like a tornado and a hurricane all at the same time. When we finally stopped, I jumped out and could barely stand up. I saw a sign that said CHIROPRACTOR and I was so happy because after that ride, I needed an adjustment!"

Today, Adele has her own anti-bullying children's book. She teaches kids to be nice to others because you never know what people are feeling on the inside and to be the best you that you can be! One of Adele's famous lines from her book is, "Be who you are, and be the very best that you can be, just like me!"

Certainly, Adele is one of the most famous animals at the Funny Farm and always teaches children that "Not being nice to others is not Not NOT okay!"

10

The Trespasser

Doing my homework in the front window one spring afternoon, I watched Stephen traipsing down the dirt path, switching a broken reed against the ground like Huck Finn, kicking stones, and dawdling as usual. He was the last one home from school that day.

I was about to call out to him when he stopped short and swung around, as if something in the woods had caught his eye. He stood very still for a moment, staring, then raced on toward the house. By the time he threw open the door, his face was chalk white and his body swayed unsteadily.

Mom walked in from the bathroom, drying her hands. "What's up?"

Without a word, he pointed toward the yard. Then he just started to wail, this high-pitched, roof-raising sound. Mom ran outside, and moments later, I heard her moan softly.

"Oh, no. Oh, no, no, no."

I followed, and there in the clearing where we kept our dogs' water and food bowls were Wolfie, Georgie, Erin, Bear, Buddy . . . All of them—a total of five dogs—lay on the ground, their bellies distended, their eyes rolled back and mouths slack. They had been poisoned.

"That son of a bitch," Mom cried. "That son of a bitch."

By then, none of us kept up the fiction that strangers had been cutting our car tires and electric lines and water hoses. We knew it was Dad. We knew it. And we knew he was the one who had done this.

But once more, no proof. And no consequences.

We dug a line of shallow graves in the rain-softened ground behind our house and laid our animals down. That's when Annie got her gun.

It wasn't more than a few weeks later that she heard the animals acting up outside, fluttering and squawking, which often meant a stranger, two-legged or four-legged, had appeared on the property. She pulled back the curtains, her mouth compressed in a vicious line, and she grabbed hold of her rifle. I didn't see what transpired next, but have heard the story often enough to feel like I witnessed it all. Mom found Dad leaning over the pasture fence, feeding a head of lettuce to Shannon O'Leary.

Like Barbara Stanwyck in some old Western movie, she cocked her rifle, a bolt-action Winchester 70, and growled, "Move away from that horse, you bastard, and get off my property. Now."

I don't know about anyone else, but if someone came at me with a rifle, I'd make a beeline. My dad was insolent. "What's the problem, sweetheart?" he asked. "I'm just trying to be friendly."

He misjudged her then, as he had misjudged her before. She pointed that barrel in the air and fired, and he jumped three feet in the air, like a cartoon character. Snarling and cussing, he took off like the coward he was—straight to the police station, where he filed a complaint, accusing his ex-wife of attempted murder.

Mom was accustomed to courts by now, and though this incident was more serious by a mile, as the story goes in our family, she faced the charges without flinching, coolly informing the judge, "If I had wanted to kill that son of a bitch, he'd be dead."

I can see and hear her saying that. I like to believe the story is true.

As a first-time offender, Mom may have gotten probation, though I wasn't privy to all the details. One thing I'm sure of, no attempted-murder charge was filed. And once again, that was that, though believe it or not, under our court-ordered visitation, we still had to visit Timber Heights Court each weekend.

The stress of it all, having to spend time with the man who had poisoned our dogs, and possibly planned to kill our horse, was more than we children could stand.

We began to quietly rebel. Many times, we would get to Dad's house, cool our heels for a couple of hours, then slip out when his back was turned and walk back home on foot. Mom, exasperated to see us heading down the dirt road to the farm, would say, "Kids, don't you know I could get arrested if you don't visit your father?"

While I tried hard not to think about what had happened to the dogs—it was over and done, there was no bringing them back—I couldn't walk through the yard or down to the bus without seeing their bowls and doghouses, the place where they had died and the field where they were buried. Every school day, I would climb the steps of the bus, snuffling into my sleeve. Maybe it would have helped if someone had asked why I was crying, but no one did. So I had to wrestle with the questions on my own.

Why didn't I think to protect my dogs?

Were they scared or in pain when they died?

Why did my father hate us so much?

There were no answers, so I tried to put it out of my mind.

It's been said that the body keeps score, and the feelings you try to ignore will make themselves known one way or another, whether you're willing to face them or not. And that's what happened next. It may have been a month after the dogs were poisoned when I woke up in the morning and noticed that one side of my face was swollen. Had I slept funny, or somehow bumped it in the middle of the night?

When I looked in the bathroom mirror, I was horrified to see that the left side of my mouth was turned down, and my eye on the same side couldn't blink. Half of my face had collapsed, until I looked like a melting ice cream cake.

As I've mentioned, Mom didn't go to the doctor herself, and rarely took us unless it was a crisis, complete with blood, loose teeth, or broken bones. But that day, all it took was one look and she was dragging me out the door, on the way to the emergency room.

After running some tests, the ER doctor diagnosed a kind of facial paralysis called Bell's palsy, whose symptoms mimic those of a stroke. The condition can strike kids as well as adults, and is most likely triggered by stress.

"Is Laurie under any specific kind of pressure lately?" the doctor asked. "At home or school?"

Mom and I exchanged glances, then nodded in unison, like a pair of bobblehead dolls.

The good news, he said, was that the paralysis was usually temporary, and would likely resolve itself in a couple of weeks. The bad news was that, until then, I had to go to school looking like something out of a Salvador Dalí painting.

It didn't help that my siblings found my condition hilarious. When I tried to eat, the food fell out of the limp side of my mouth. I had to drink from a straw on the side that worked, and when I laughed or yawned or grimaced, the expression registered on that side only. Worst of all, I drooled constantly. But, as the doctor promised, I soon recovered.

I also recovered from loving my father. For years, I had made excuses for his crimes. Now, like my mother and sister before me, I heard that interior door slam and lock tight. On weekends, I no longer returned his hugs or gripped his arm in that possessive way. I was also less afraid of him than I had been before, as if some hex had been broken.

The next time the three of us kids went to family court, Cathy stood calmly before the bench and told the judge, "If we have to go to our father's house, we will just turn around and go back home."

She didn't say it in a petulant way—it was just the facts, ma'am.

That time, thankfully, the judge heard her. She knew our family's history of sometimes violent disputes. She knew the mom-on-the-Cadillac story, which had become legendary around Turnersville. On that day, the judge and the court heard the voices of Richard Zaleski's children. Just like that, we were allowed to declare our emancipation. We were freed of the obligation to spend weekends at Timber Heights Court. Only Stephen continued to see Dad. He still enjoyed their visits, and we were okay with that. But Cathy and me? We were finished.

Unaccustomed to defiance, Dad fought back with all the venom he could muster. He accused Mom of being an unfit parent, of raising his children in squalor, even of being a drug dealer. But he couldn't prove it, because it wasn't true. He swore that if he was unable to see his daughters, he was goddamned if he would pay for their support.

Mom's wasn't impressed. She probably wanted to strangle him—I know I did—but all she said was, "I don't need any help from you. Please let this be over. Just leave us in peace."

One momentous day in 1980, Mom came home bursting with an announcement that would change all our lives for the better: "Kids, I'm a teamster!"

Barney had lucked into a good-paying union job at the UPS warehouse in Philadelphia, then helped her get in, too. She'd been hired as a "pre-loader," or package handler, to work the loading dock on the graveyard shift.

For the first time in her life, Mom told us, she would make decent money. Overtime. Double time. Golden time, whatever that was. She would also get a great benefits package, meaning we could actually go to the doctor if we got sick.

Waltzing through the living room, she grabbed a stack of blue shut-off notices from the electric company, ripped them to shreds, and tossed them in the air like confetti. That week, she took us out to a real restaurant, not a drive-through, and said don't worry about the cost—at least, not much. And that weekend, in a fit of indulgence, she drove us all to the mall to buy new clothes.

Ironically, it was just about this time that I adopted a sort of run-down, Raggedy Ann style of dress, because that's how I thought artists should look. I paired shit-kicker boots with slouch socks, off-beat hats, and *Flashdance*-style sweatshirts. I stacked rubber bracelets up and down my arms, wore mesh gloves, wore underwear as outerwear, deliberately ripped holes in my tights, and tried hard to kink my long blonde hair. Just when we could afford nice clothes, I looked like I'd escaped from a road show of *Godspell*.

And while the look was cheap, as often as not, the clothes weren't. I'd been babysitting for pocket money since I was eleven, and now I stepped it up, working nights, weekends, sometimes overnights, as much as I could, to support my shopping mania. I also got an after-school job, doing weeding at a nearby optician's office, the Spectacle Shoppe, where Cathy did some filing.

The owner, George DuBois, was a stern and exacting boss. He would actually hover over me as I weeded the speck of green outside his front door, picking apart my technique, and pointing out dandelion sprouts that I'd overlooked. There was nothing I hated more than weeding, and now I had to put up with his haranguing, too.

I did it, just to get the paycheck.

What I couldn't know then was that George would become an important person in my life, Cathy's life, and all our lives: an employer, a constant benefactor, and an enduring friend. But even at the start, if I ran short of cash and needed anything—from new shoes to school and art supplies to field trip money—I learned I could go to him.

His response never varied. First came the eye-rolling, then the grumbling. "Broke again? Are you kidding? And what do you think I am, the First National Bank?" But, invariably, once he was done kvetching, George would find a way to help me. Always.

"Well, there's some weeding out there with your name on it . . ."

From that point on, Dr. George was affectionately known in my family as "the Bank."

Happily, he soon moved me out of those hated weeds and into the store office, where I did low-level administrative work: filing, keeping the appointment calendar updated, answering phones. Because of my art expertise, in time, he promoted me to "fashion consultant," helping his customers choose the eyeglass frames, colors, and styles that would be most becoming to them. His customers were chiefly middle-aged and older men and women, so why he trusted this job to someone who looked like a suburban-mall Madonna, I'll never know. But I loved it—not just the money, but the feeling of independence.

Mom, too, loved her new job. There weren't many women pre-loaders at the Philadelphia warehouse, and only a handful in her chapter of the International Brotherhood of Teamsters. She was so proud to have made the cut, to be a chick doing men's work and earning men's wages.

But her kids sure weren't surprised. Hadn't she been doing heavy-duty, physical labor for years? It was nothing to her to round up a runaway stallion or wrestle a thousand-pound hog. She split logs like a lumberjack and then chopped them into kindling. Hefting forty-pound packages didn't faze her a bit. She was as strong as most of the guys, maybe stronger, and could load and unload the trucks just as quickly, if not more, than they did.

Whatever her male colleagues thought the day Anne McNulty showed up for her first shift, they soon realized that she was a stud. They liked her, and respected her tenacity. When they learned a bit about her background and the husband who continued to harass her, they became protective of her, and angry on her behalf. What kind of jerk would bother a nice gal like Annie?

My father was less of a menace by then—he couldn't be, with Barney in the picture—but damned if he didn't keep at it, and most times managed to come and go without being seen. When Mom's tires were slashed yet again and paint thrown on the car, this time in the parking lot of the UPS terminal, her teamster buds were outraged. More than once, they discreetly offered to "take care" of Dad in exchange for a couple of six-packs.

"C'mon, Annie," they told her. "We can get him gone. Or at least, let us knock some sense into him."

But once again, Mom refused. "What goes around, comes around," she said. "Two wrongs don't make a right."

All in all, that was a happy time, a fairly peaceful, golden time, until the defining event my brother Stephen calls Dad's "finale." It came in 1983. Four of us were at home—Stephen, Gordon, Mom, and me. Cathy was at a sleepover. Barney must have been at work.

Only Stephen heard the gunfire—one pop, then another—which awakened him in the early-morning hours, about half past two. He sat up in bed and squinted into the darkness, listening hard. Then, silence. Hearing nothing more, he lay back down and dozed off again until six o'clock, when Mom opened the door of his room. Pushing his shoulder, she said in a rough voice, "Get up right now, and help me. Shannon's dead."

The raised voices woke me, and I came yawning out of my room to see Mom, pale and resolute as she pushed open the back door.

"Laurie, get dressed and grab a shovel," she said. "Somebody killed Shannon. We have to bury him."

Over her shoulder, I locked eyes with Stephen, who was wide-eyed and too shocked to cry, and Gordon, who trailed behind him, openmouthed.

I fell apart. Of all the animals on our farm, Shannon was my favorite, my true love. It was unrequited love, to be sure—the more I adored him, the more he rejected me, sort of like a bad boyfriend. Over the years he had nipped me and kicked me. Any time I tried to ride him, he'd thrown me off into the dirt. It had never stopped me from loving him.

And so that morning I stumbled after Mom and Stephen, sobbing uncontrollably, so much so that I started to hyperventilate. Mom wasn't having it. Straightaway she got in my face and hollered, "Laurie, I do not have time for this crap right now! Suck it up and help us, or go back in the house!"

I was hurt that she would berate me at a moment like that, but that was Mom's way, her armor. She was stoic in the face of calamity.

Shovels in hand, we reached the pasture. There lay Shannon, in a heap on the grass, his legs extended and his body already stiffening. I began to blubber again, but one look from Mom, and I quickly got it under control.

He had come to us as a foal, homeless, injured, and struggling to survive. We had seen him take his first tentative steps. We had watched him learn to walk, then to run, then to run away, looking for love in a pasture down the road. He had been high-spirited and beautiful. Now Shannon was dead, killed with two gunshots, one to the temple, another behind the ear.

Mom was expressionless as we dug his grave, one shovelful of earth at a time, until his grave was about four feet deep. Then we laid an old car hood upside-down on the grass, pushed Shannon's body on top, chained the old hood to my MG, and dragged it like a sled to the grave. There, Shannon would rest with all the other animals we'd buried over the years—Wolfie, Erin, Georgie, and all the rest.

The police took it pretty seriously this time, photographing footprints found in the pasture and collecting the bullet casings. They performed a gun trace and determined that the shots had come from a .38 caliber revolver loaded with flat-headed bullets called wad-cutters. While they're typically used for target practice and are not really accurate at a distance, wad-cutters can be deadly at close range. And in this case, they sure had been.

I'll give you something to cry about.

It was one of the most sorrowful days of my life, but I would never see another one like it. After years of terror and intimidation, with one final, vicious act, my father must have felt he had evened the score. Like the villain in a play, he took a bow, made his exit, and vanished completely from our lives.

I would encounter him once, fleetingly, a few years after Shannon died. But we wouldn't speak again for more than twenty-five years.

With a mom like ours, all of us kids, Gordon included, learned resilience and a strong work ethic. We absorbed it, in our bones, in our blood. Like her, we grew calluses and independence. I like to think we inherited some of her courage. We became consummate bootstrappers: industrious, and maybe a little headstrong.

In the mid-1990s, we also became activists. That's when Mom single-handedly mounted a campaign to save a tree on the Black Horse Pike.

The ancient red oak was immense: almost a hundred feet tall and measuring sixteen feet around the middle. By some accounts, the tree was more than two hundred years old, and had been growing in that field since the signing of the Declaration of Independence.

But when plans were approved to develop a shopping center along the pike, including a Walmart and a Sam's Club discount store, the tree was tagged to come down, along with a twenty-one-acre wooded tract of land.

Mom was dismayed. She knew she couldn't stop the development itself, but she didn't understand why the tree had to go, too. "Just let it stand," she wrote, in a letter to the local paper. "Let it be a nice place where people can sit, relax, and be reminded of nature."

That was just the start. She drew up a petition to save the tree,

in hopes of gathering a couple hundred signatures. She didn't realize how many others felt as she did. The campaign quickly caught
on, and generated a ton of press. Copies of the petition were circulated in person, through the mail, at local stores, from neighbor to neighbor. This was long before the internet became widely
available; for Mom, it was all legwork and phone work. She wrote
impassioned appeals to local and state politicians, including then-
Governor Jim Florio. She even sought help from Hillary Clinton,
who was First Lady at the time and a former board member at
Walmart, an Arkansas-based company.

Mom's next move was to mount a demonstration along the
Black Horse Pike, near the field where the old tree lived. One of
her many scrapbooks includes photos and newspaper clippings
of crowds marching up and down the highway, in and out of traffic, with signs that read SAVE IT, DON'T PAVE IT. We kids were front
and center, and helped protestors who wreathed the tree in yellow
ribbons. A newspaper photo shows her hanging a sign on the tree
trunk that reads SAVE ME.

Our old friend Jimmy Bacon joined the fight, too. By then,
he lived in the resort town of Wildwood, where he worked as a
bartender. Jimmy circulated Mom's petition at the bar, and his
patrons were only too happy to sign, even though Wildwood is
almost an hour down south. It seemed that people throughout
South Jersey grew to love that mighty oak, and feel passionate
about its survival.

By the time the campaign was through, more than 3,000 people
had signed that petition. I guess that's when Walmart realized it
would win a lot more friends—and future customers—by sparing
the tree. It wasn't a big loss anyway—it would only mean fifteen
fewer parking spaces on a lot that contained hundreds. Even so,
the whole effort took two exhausting years, and our mother—
Mother Nature—never waved the white flag.

"It's a matter of principle," she said to us. "You've got to decide what you believe in, and stand up for those things."

The tree huggers had triumphed. The tree got a reprieve. We threw a party to celebrate.

But shortly thereafter, in the overnight hours, someone crept into the field with a chainsaw and gouged a six-inch swath around the tree trunk. The technique is called girdling, and a local environmentalist compared it to slashing a vein. With girdling, nutrients cannot travel from the leaves to the roots, and the tree slowly starves. There was nothing that could be done. Mom was heartsick.

Meanwhile, the developer of the land griped that my mom's campaign had delayed groundbreaking on the shopping center by six months. An area councilman agreed, and said the Walmart would have opened much sooner "if not for the ballyhoo made for the tree."

Not surprisingly, the new shopping center kicked off a trend of commercial development on the Black Horse Pike that eventually flattened miles and miles of rural terrain, destroyed thousands of acres of trees, and turned all that wilderness into shopping centers, supermarkets, malls, and car dealerships. The area is almost unrecognizable today.

Over the years, Barney had continued his hard-drinking ways, and bit by bit, it began to show in his health and appearance as well as his temperament. He was no longer lean and handsome but red-faced and puffy. His behavior became even more erratic, as the following incident shows.

As a teenager, I monopolized the phone and it irritated him to no end. I'd take the receiver and stretch the long cord from the kitchen into the bathroom. There, I'd perch on the toilet seat and gab for hours with my friends, keeping the door shut with my foot. I also did my homework in there, to the point that Mom called the bathroom "Laurie's office."

Barney fumed. He said, rightly so, that it was inconsiderate of me to tie up the phone and monopolize the bathroom. But I was a teenager, and I didn't care—until the morning he blew his stack. It started when he walked through the kitchen and straight into that stretched-out cord, which caught him under the chin like a noose.

He went off like a powder keg. First, he yanked on the phone cord until the receiver flew out of my hand and I fell off the toilet seat. Then he ripped the whole phone off the kitchen wall, and tossed the receiver into a hot frying pan, where it sizzled, along with the eggs and bacon, until the earpiece melted.

Later on, both of us—me and Barney—had to face Mom and explain why there was a hole in the kitchen wall and a melted phone stuck to the frying pan. She was mighty unhappy, and dressed both of us down as if we were unruly toddlers.

As Cathy and I got older and went from skinny adolescents to budding teens, Barney felt free to compare us, saying right to our faces that she was the smart one and I was the pretty one. It was unfair to us both to be pigeonholed that way. Cathy, while smart as a whip, was no plain Jane—for crying out loud, she looked like Mom, the woman he loved! And though I was "flaky Laurie," the Barbie blonde, I considered myself smart, too.

Maybe worst of all, when he was in his cups, Barney didn't mind making suggestive comments to us girls. Any time either one of us had to inch past him in that cramped kitchen, almost belly to belly, he'd say: "Excuse me or squeeze me."

It made my blood boil, and I sucked it up for a long time before lashing back. Then came the point that one time I shot back, "Why don't I kick you in the balls and be done with it?"

He also installed a peephole in our bedroom door; we only had to try it once to know it had been installed the wrong way—for peeping in, not peeping out. He claimed it was unintentional. Did he think we were simpletons?

Mom really loved Barney, and it took her way too long to be done with him for keeps. She would draw a line, forbid certain behaviors, he would test her resolve, and she would redraw the line. That was the pattern, long into our teens. The end came the day he crawled onto the roof of a corrugated tin shed behind our house, we think with the intent of peering in the bathroom window as Cathy showered.

It was instant karma. The tin was rusted through, and Barney was probably loaded. When he took a misstep, he fell through to the ground, breaking his ankle. It was his downfall in more ways than one. Mom exploded like dynamite, and he was out of there, no questions or explanations, in the next twenty-four hours. On crutches.

In one huge way, my mother was *not* my role model, and that was how she bent her will to the will of two men, first my father and then Barney. How could she escape the tyranny of that marriage, then crawl under the thumb of another man? How could she be so independent on one hand, yet so submissive on the other? It perplexed me then, it perplexes me now, and I have no doubt it influenced the way I often feel when a relationship gets too close—like a wild horse, being broken to the saddle. The thought of being controlled that way makes me want to jump the fence.

Having grown up as we did, perhaps it's no surprise that Cathy, Stephen, and I all have been married and divorced. And though I won't speak for them, any time anyone in my life tries to be the boss, I start looking for the exit.

I am independent to a fault, and I mean that in a literal sense— very often I wish I could yield a little bit, compromise more. But

having seen the subjugation of my mother in her own home—
and, frankly, her complicity in it—I'm almost phobic about these
things. I bristle at the thought of someone living my life for me.
When one of my boyfriends offered me an engagement ring, I
asked for a skid-steer loader instead. "It'll come in handy around
the farm." And he brought it home for me on a flatbed Christmas
Eve. That's love. Red roses? Boxes of candy? For some people, the
quickest road to their heart is farm equipment.

I've joked to friends that relationships should come with a seven-
year escape clause. At the end of the term, you re-up or let it lapse.
Like a Get Out of Jail Free card. There's an old Dolly Parton song
that sums up my feelings about it: "I'll be movin' on when possession gets too strong."

That said, I'm still friendly with my ex-husband, Frank, a Master Sergeant in the Air Force and an awfully nice guy. And what
do you know—our marriage lasted just about seven years.

One day soon after Barney left, I was in a department store with
my then-boyfriend, Joe, when I noticed a man at one of the check-
out lines. What he was checking out was me.

I was about eighteen at the time, and it would have been hard to
miss me. I had grown to my full height of five feet ten inches, and
I looked like a Barbie doll come to life: big boobs, narrow waist,
long blonde hair. The way I looked wasn't any kind of invitation—it
was just the way I looked. But I couldn't escape it, and I had grown
accustomed to getting the once-over from guys, the "hey-baby"
stare, sometimes wolf whistles and crude comments. I didn't mind
the attention, and I could always handle myself.

But this man really creeped me out. For one thing, he was
clearly much older. For another, he was so cocksure, sweeping me
up and down with his eyes, grinning all the while.

I returned the stare with one of my own, a dirty look that said, "Who do you think you are, jerk?"

That's when I felt it—a jolt of recognition. I whirled around, grabbed on to Joe's arm, and dragged him toward the exit, muttering, "Get me *outta here* . . ."

"What's the matter, Laurie?" Joe asked, out in the parking lot. "Did you know that man?"

"Unfortunately, yes, I know him. Joe, that was my father."

Animal Tails

Ricky and Lucy

In my view, peacock wrangling could be a spectator sport. It sure draws a crowd, and when I was trying to round up Ricky and Lucy, I wish I could have charged admission.

It was a few years ago when I got the call that two peacocks, a male and a female (more correctly, a peacock and a peahen), were wandering the grounds of a condo development in Mays Landing. Apparently, they were doing just fine, living on bugs, berries, and plants. They could have survived that way indefinitely. But as I've mentioned, peacocks make a blood-curdling noise: their high-volume screech carries for miles, especially during mating season. And that was never going to pass muster with the condo association.

Catching them wasn't easy or quick, because they can fly. Over the course of a few weeks, Cathy and I and a couple of friends made repeated attempts to capture the pair, chasing them through the condo community with giant nets. We always attracted a crowd, mostly condo residents, who watched like it was the Super Bowl. Some brought popcorn and laughed at each play.

In this game, the peacocks were the home team. Every time we inched close enough to bring down the nets they just flew away, and many of the residents cheered. Some wanted to see them go because they kept pooping on their decks. Again, the birds would lift off and float down nearby, and it was on to the next play, or down, or whatever they call it in football.

Finally, I got the bright idea to stash some food under one of the condo decks, in hopes of corralling them that way. It worked like a charm. I went out one morning at four—the bleachers were empty at that hour—then crawled under the deck, knowing they would be asleep. And score! I nabbed both Ricky and Lucy before they could get away, placed them both in large crates, and took them home. It was all about timing.

The loving couple settled in nicely at the farm, but disaster struck when Lucy crossed Railroad Boulevard to lay her eggs, and Ricky followed. He is bright white, magnificent, and certainly hard to miss among the pines, but out in the country, people drive like there's no speed limit, no other people or animals. He was hit. I rushed him to the veterinary hospital, where an X-ray revealed that he had a broken spinal vertebra.

"Sorry, Laurie, but he won't recover," said the vet. "With his spine broken, he will never walk or fly again—It'd be best to put him down."

I choked back the tears when I heard the news. "Well, is he in any pain? Can I take him home to say goodbye to Lucy?"

"He's probably not in too much discomfort. Go ahead, and bring him back in a couple of days when you're ready."

On the way home, with Ricky riding in my lap, I got to thinking. Okay, if he isn't in a lot of pain, why rush to put him down?

By the time we got home, I'd already sketched out a plan in my head.

First, I put Ricky in the bottom half of a dog crate lined with soft straw and he lived in my kitchen for the next three months while I built him his new digs. The plan would be to buy a corn-crib, which is a large, round, cage-like bin with a roof for storing ears of corn. The large, round cage construction would ensure proper ventilation and space for the two birds. I found a used one for sale nearby. With help from some friends, I disassembled it, brought it home on a trailer, and reassembled it. My plan was to put a harness on Ricky, with a bungee cord attached to the top of the corncrib. It would allow him to sit comfortably, slightly elevated, with his body supported but his legs and feet hanging freely—sort of like one of those bouncy-baby things that look like so much fun. (Why don't they make those for grown-ups?)

During the corncrib construction, Ricky was in his temporary crate in my kitchen, next to the sliding glass door. Every day Lucy would come to the back porch to visit him through the glass door. I would slide the door open and let the sweethearts sit next to each other, and for a few months that was our daily routine.

Then came the day I put Ricky in the bathtub to clean the scrape on his back. While he was in the water, I saw one of his legs kick out like a swimmer's. Ecstatic, I shouted out like a TV preacher, "He's healed! He was paralyzed, but now he's healed! It's a miracle!"

Encouraged, I began a more active rehab program. Each day as I changed Ricky's bedding, I would lift and lower him in hopes of strengthening his legs. Then I took him outside, and did the same exercises in the grass. It took two months, but finally he stood up all on his own. In a few more days, he stood up and took a step before sitting back down. The next week, he took a few more faltering steps, then spread his wings and flew across the front yard, ending with a chest skid—just the way Sully safely landed that big plane on the Hudson River. I couldn't believe my eyes! Each day his improvement was remarkable until he was completely recovered.

Ricky's miraculous comeback taught me an important lesson. Many times, I've had animals whose recovery seemed unlikely, for whom vets recommended euthanasia as the most compassionate choice.

But when I think of Ricky, I always think twice.

Today, at least four generations of Ricky and Lucy's kin—the whole Ricardo family—live at the Funny Farm. I wish I could report that the lovebirds are still together, but peacocks mate for a season, not for life. As soon as I got some blue peacocks, Lucy ran off. That little hussy.

Ricky, too, has met some new peahens by strutting his stuff with his unique, beautiful white and blue feathers. He now flies around the farm like he owns the place. Ricky's healing was a true Funny Farm miracle, one of many.

11

The Good Fight

No one in the family expected poky, flaky Laurie to become a successful businesswoman. Least of all me. But I'd always been a hard worker, believing in the axiom espoused by Mom, "The harder I work, the luckier I'll get." And when I hit a professional speed bump—one that could've derailed my career before it started—I had the world's greatest cheerleader. You know who.

For almost ten years, I'd continued to work for George DuBois at the Spectacle Shoppe, on the fast track from weed patrol to fashion consultant to lens grinder. Eventually, George sent me to optical sciences school, hoping to add me to his staff full-time.

I was tempted by the offer, which came with an astronomical salary of forty thousand dollars a year. But deep down, I knew I didn't want to be an optician. Dr. George was stupefied when I thanked him for the opportunity, then turned it down.

"Please understand," I said. "I'm an artist. If I can't be that, I don't want to be anything."

He was irked, but hugged me and wished me all the best.

I had won a summer scholarship at Moore College of Art in Philadelphia to study illustration, and by the time I was nineteen, had formed a one-woman company, Laurie Zaleski Inc. And wouldn't you know, dear old Dr. George was behind my first big break. He called an acquaintance who knew someone who had a contact at Campbell Soup in Camden. That got me an interview for a job in the art department, and a great ongoing gig as a freelance artist.

I felt so grand and grown-up driving into the company headquarters. Its water tower, visible for miles, looked like a giant red-and-white soup can with the Campbell's brand name in that famous gold script. It was a prestigious job and paid a princely ten bucks an hour—a fortune in my eyes. I think my teachers at Moore were a little irked at me for landing such a good job so early in my career.

Back then, most illustration was still done by hand, and I was in my element. For example, I was responsible for creating the coupons for Swanson's "Great Starts" microwave breakfasts. The art had to be lifelike, photorealistic, yet it was all done with stippling: using a series of hand-rendered colored dots to make up the larger image. I took a sort of Zen-like pleasure in leaning over my light table, drawing hundreds of thousands of tiny dots that ended up looking like French toast and syrup and strips of bacon.

But I was smart enough to recognize the future of computer graphics and actively prepare for it. Some of my contemporaries resisted computers, saying they were the beginning of the end of "real art." But I didn't agree. Though I loved drawing by hand, I embraced the digital age. Everything at Moore was old-school, everything was done on the drawing board. After finishing the summer program there, I got a full ride to Glassboro State College, now Rowan University, and learned programs like SuperPaint, PaintBox—all the precursors of the design tools we use today. It was a smart choice and gave me a decided edge in the job market.

My first full-time job out of school was for a contractor at McGuire Air Force Base in Wrightstown. I was an entry-level graphic designer, making even bigger bucks—more than eleven dollars an hour. I thought I had arrived. And with all that dough, I felt like Rockefeller.

Then came the speed bump. It started when my bosses transferred me from McGuire to another government agency. They promoted me to manager—a good sign—but actually cut my pay by about one-third.

It was a weird sort of promotion-demotion. When I objected, they assured me I'd soon be raised back to my former rate, but months passed, and nothing changed. After a year, when we had a meeting about it again, they basically said, "Sorry, blondie, it's not in our budget."

That's when Mom got mad—first at my employers, who thought they could double-cross and underpay a woman, and then at me, for accepting the unacceptable.

"Laurie, you go after these people. Tell them a deal's a deal."

"It was a verbal agreement, Mom, a handshake." I sighed. "There's no way I can prove they broke their word. I'm screwed."

Wrong answer. "And what, I ask you, is more binding than a handshake? As for breaking their word—isn't that also known as *lying?*" This really got Annie's Irish up. "Now stop your sniveling," she scolded me. "You're my daughter, and I think I raised you better than to lie down and take it. You keep after those people until you get your rights."

I'd love to say I rode right into battle, like Joan of Arc, but I quaked at the thought of confronting my bosses. So I turned for advice to a friend who understood government contracting. To my surprise, he seemed less concerned than puzzled.

"Laurie," he said, "all you've got to do is bid against the contractor"—in other words, go up for the job against the people who had hired me.

"I can do that?"

"Of course you can. It's an open bidding process. If you're qualified—and I think you are—then apply for the contract yourself."

Even then, I hesitated to take such a bold step, and tried one more time to make peace with my employers. I approached them with a proposal: I would stay on as their manager, but only if they honored their word and raised my hourly rate back to what it had been. Otherwise, they could consider me a competitor.

"You don't have to do it right away, just give me a quarter to start," I said. "All I want to know is that we're moving in the right direction."

If they had agreed, it's possible I would be running their company today. But they dismissed me. I think in their view, because I looked like a twentysomething Barbie doll, I wasn't to be taken seriously. I was inconsequential. A beginner who could be easily bamboozled.

But I had two things going for me: my mother, who would probably have disowned me if I had given in, and pride, both in my work ethic and my ability. I worked up a bid for the graphic arts contract. And I lost.

At that point, I would have felt justified giving up. But darn it, I knew my offer was competitive and my package was good, so I asked to compare the two bids, as was my right. I was floored to discover that, when it came to key personnel requirements, the incumbents had ranked zero, which should have knocked them out of the bidding from the start. My proposal ranked ten in every category. It was my "gotcha" moment.

The government quickly acknowledged its error, but instead of awarding me the contract, offered me a settlement instead. I was mighty tempted. It was decent money at a time when I couldn't even make my car payments. But I didn't want a payoff. I wanted the contract. I refused the offer.

Surprised at my persistence, the government agreed I would be hired the following year. But when the time came, the offer was rescinded. After a two-year fight that had practically given me an ulcer, I was through.

"It's time to put my toys away and go home," I told Mom. "I can't take it anymore."

"Before you quit," she said, "ask yourself if you know you're right, if this contract is rightfully yours."

"Mom, *please* don't do the whole pep-talk thing again. Something's up with these people. They have the inside track. I can't beat them."

"You didn't answer my question. Do you know, deep down, that you're right?"

I slumped at the kitchen table. "Yes. I know I'm right."

"Do you know that you're *one hundred percent right*?"

"Yes, damn it, yes!"

"Well, then. Be the woman I raised you to be. You fight those people."

"I'd need a lawyer at this point, and I have no money." I actually opened my wallet. "See? Cobwebs."

"The Bank will lend it to us."

"And what if I don't win?"

"At least you'll know you gave it your all, and you won't look back with any regrets."

Long story short, with her encouragement and a loan from George ("You need a loan? I've got some weeding for you"), I hired a lawyer, prepared a legal case, and with my little slingshot, brought down Goliath. I won the government contract in 1998, and my business, since renamed Art-Z Graphics, has been working in government contracts ever since, doing graphic design, photography, and multimedia. My staff and I have created murals that hang in the White House. I've photographed Air Force One and all the presidents who've held the office since I won the contract. I've come a far piece, and, today, my mom would be thrilled with how far I've come. I've also taken aerial photos for the Coast Guard, hanging halfway out of a helicopter while tethered in a flight suit. I've flown with the U.S. Army Golden Knights parachute team in their big C-141 Starlifters, shooting in-flight photos of their magnificent jumps and aerobatics.

Once so terrified of heights, I now hang out of helicopters and airplanes.

I dreamed myself into a wonderful life, imagining and sketching out my future, like Harold and the Purple Crayon. I was a working artist with a rewarding job and a team of wonderful employees. It was on to the next dream.

First, I would fulfill the promise I'd made as a girl: to buy a real farm for my mother, where she could retire and rescue animals full-time.

As for me, I'd live in bohemian splendor, an urban cowgirl in an artist's loft, like Demi Moore in the movie *Ghost*. My loft would have the same vaulted ceilings and skylights, the same kiln and pottery wheel and of course, Patrick Swayze, or the South Philly/ South Jersey equivalent.

After a lifetime of never enough, I wanted more than enough, in both my professional and personal lives. Buoyed by my new contract, I started buying *stuff*, shiny new evidence of my prosperity, and wasted no time getting into hock. First came a sporty new convertible. Then a secondhand Harley-Davidson. Then a vintage 1965 Austin-Healey Sprite Mark IV, my favorite car on earth. Then a closetful of smart business clothes, watches, and jewelry. Those were what Mom called my highfalutin days.

"You're living high on the hog," she said. "But hogs are slippery. You just might slide off, right into the slop."

"It wouldn't be anything new," I said.

I understood what she said, but listened with half an ear. I was young and brash, full of big plans, successful in my career, and loaded with new credit.

At work, I was CEO Barbie in my couture suits and high heels. But at home, I was still Elly May Clampett, in jeans and shit-kickers, helping Mom feed those slippery swine.

The property around the Funny Farm had changed. Developers had mowed down all the apple and peach trees to make way for a medical complex. The Hitcharama now extended way back to the fields where we used to play, and the lot was crowded with monster RVs and camper vans. A lot of the wilderness was gone, and with it went some of the deer and foxes, the bees and butterflies. There was more traffic noise.

Those crazy hippie guys who had lived in trailers down near the highway were history, of course, and so was the Afternoon Delight. For all that, we were still fairly secluded back there, with plenty of fields for our animals to live and play.

In more than a quarter century, our landlord Mr. Clark had only raised the rent to three hundred dollars—still dirt-cheap—with the stipulation that we do our own repairs. It was the deal of the century, and every one of us was handy, so with a little help from our friends we took on each job, big and small, from digging a new well to replacing the roof. We installed a new set of front steps and put in an electric fence to keep the animals safe at home.

I still fantasized about the day I'd buy my mother a real farm, but until that time, she was content to stay put and never considered moving. By her reckoning, why pay market rate for a condo or apartment when she could stay right where she was, in what was left of the backwoods?

In the end, though, it always came down to the animals.

"If I move, who will take care of them?" Mom asked. "Besides, I'm happy here. And now that the other kids have moved out, doesn't this place feel really huge? It's like a castle."

I got a charge out of getting her off the farm, treating her to shopping sprees and four-star restaurants and summer vacations. Her favorite outing ever was to see *Man of La Mancha* in Philadelphia, starring her all-time favorite, Robert Goulet. I splurged on the tickets—fifth or sixth row, orchestra—and she was beyond excited. Throughout the show she was on the edge of her seat, and when the time came for Don Quixote's anthem, "The Impossible Dream," I had to poke her in the ribs to keep her from sobbing out loud.

Afterward, she was determined to get her idol's autograph.

"We'll ambush him at the stage door."

"Jeez, Mom, do we *hafta*? This is Robert *Goulet*, not Robert Plant."

But she was as giddy as a schoolgirl at the thought of meeting him in person, so we loitered with a few other fans in the alleyway behind the Merriam Theater until he emerged, a cashmere coat slung over his arm, almost glowing with star quality, with his matinee-idol looks and velvety baritone. Robert Goulet was very warm and friendly, but I was red-faced to see my mom hanging on her heartthrob like a groupie.

"Laurie, take our picture!" she commanded, and handed me her ever-present Kodak. I took a couple of shots that make me smile to see today: Mom yakking in his ear as he gazes at the camera, a bemused smile on that Lancelot face.

After meeting Robert Goulet, she was in seventh heaven, cloud nine. "Now I can die happy," she said.

* * *

I made my most extravagant purchase during a vacation in the Virgin Islands, when my boyfriend and I agreed to take a "free" rum cruise—free, if we listened to a sales pitch for time shares. Before long, I was signing on the dotted line, committing myself to a lease that didn't expire until the twelfth of never. I was the proud owner of one-fifty-second of a resort property.

But it was a glorious setting, at Hotel on the Cay in St. Croix, on an islet off the historic town of Christiansted. Every room had a mesmerizing ocean view.

Part of the charm was that we had to take a ferry from our hotel tower to reach the main island, where we always headed for dinner and drinks. For me, it was a special joy to see Mom in such lovely surroundings: the picturesque Caribbean with its soft, ivory beaches and waving palms and sailboats gliding by on aqua seas. We went snorkeling, diving, and sailing. She took a million and one photos to add to her growing stack of scrapbooks.

For one week a year—my turn came in September—I was Lady Bountiful and treated my family and friends to a vacation in paradise. They descended like locusts, but I didn't care. I was like Mom that way—the more the merrier. If they could afford the flight, they were welcome to come and stay. Sometimes we jammed seven or eight people into that little place.

One day on Cay Beach, lounging in a bikini with a piña colada, my mother raised the frosty glass in a toast. "If I could stop time, I'd do it right here and now." She pulled out a maraschino cherry and popped it in her mouth. "This is the life."

By that time, Barney had been out of the picture for a few years, and on vacation, my mother and I switched roles: she became the girl, and I the disapproving parent.

At a bar on Christiansted, she met a handsome man named

Brian, and instantly, sparks flew. She liked his square jaw, square shoulders, and an all-around James Garner vibe. He was quite taken with her, too. My mom was still young, only forty-seven at the time, curvy, bubbly, the life of every party. If anything, she was even more dazzled when Brian let slip that he was an FBI agent.

The early disclosure made me skeptical. "He spilled that little tidbit pretty quick, didn't he, Mom? I'm thinking Brian wouldn't make a very good counterspy."

"Maybe not," Mom agreed, "but he sure can limbo!"

Of all people, I understood my mother's need to kick up her heels. But one night, when she didn't return to the resort as planned, I started to worry. Alternately fretting and fuming, I watched as the clock ticked off the hours. Three o'clock. Four o'clock. Five frickin' o'clock. I must have dozed off around sunrise, then woke when I heard the key in the door. It was mid-morning. Mom sailed in, still in her party dress and sparkling earrings, with a beatific smile on her face. I lost it.

"Well now! Here she comes, walking the walk of shame! Could you have at least called, so I wouldn't think you were dead in some alley?" I cringed to hear my shrewish tone, but I'd been genuinely worried, and now was genuinely ticked off. "For all I knew, you could have been stuffed in an oil drum and sold into the sex trade. These things happen, you know."

Dropping her purse on the sofa, she drifted to the balcony and held out her arms, like a benediction. "What a glorious day!" She came over and gave me a brief hug. "Missed the last ferry, sorry. He's handsome, isn't he?"

How could I stay mad at her? When it came to romance, her life had been zero fun—one brief, turbulent marriage followed by one long, troubled relationship. That morning, she had a glow in her cheeks. She was carefree, with sun-streaked curls and lightly tanned skin that brought out her Irish freckles. Even as I scowled at her, I thought she looked beautiful, and for the first time, realized that if I could connect the dots, the six freckles on the bridge of her nose would form a star.

"All right already!" I sighed. "Go ahead and be the teenager this time. I guess it's long overdue."

And on the phone that night, I was able to laugh with Cathy about babysitting our mother.

Once I resigned as chaperone and safety monitor, both of us had a lot more fun. My mother took off dancing with Brian and, as usual, made dozens of other friends among the islanders and hotel guests.

Near the end of our vacation, we finally caught up for dinner. Mom looked pretty in a navy summer dress with a tiny daisy print—daisies, her favorite flower. Afterward, relaxed and happy, we headed out to the ferry terminal, and were halfway across the restaurant parking lot when she fell out of step. I turned around to see her clutching her stomach as blood streamed down her legs.

"Jesus! Mom! What's going on?"

For a split second in the lamplight, I thought I saw fear in her eyes. In the next split second it was gone, and she was waving her hand dismissively. "No, no, no. Nothing, it's nothing. Menopause, I think." She smiled wryly. "'Female complaint,' they used to call it. Don't give it a thought."

"What do you mean, menopause? How long has this been going on?"

"Not long. A couple months. I'll go to the doctor when we get home. Come on, we'll miss the ferry."

We walked on for a few minutes, then she gasped and doubled over. Out came another gush of blood, so much that I felt a little woozy. To my horror, she reached under her dress, yanked off her bloody panties, and knelt down, trying to scrub her own blood off the dark surface of the parking lot.

"Mom, for crying out loud! You don't have to do that."

"A mess," she fussed, and scrubbed harder, her head bent to the surface of the lot. "I've made a real mess."

We boarded the ferry, and she carefully spread her shawl on the seat before she sat down. In the darkness I could still see the blood, glistening sticky and wet on her legs. We rode halfway across Gallows Bay in silence before I asked quietly, "Hey, Mom? What happened back there?"

She fixed her gaze on the shore. "Female problems, that's all. I said I'll see a doctor."

"Do you promise?"

"I promise. Now stop your worrying."

And so I tried to forget that troubling image: my mother on her knees in a darkened parking lot, trying to scrub away her own blood.

Animal Tails

Road Show

And now, dear reader, kindly send the kiddies off to play as I recount one of the most memorable (and X-rated) rescues in the history of the original Funny Farm.

In my early twenties, only Mom and me remained in that tiny house. Cathy had married and worked in the marketing department at Boeing (Barney was a mechanic there, and helped her get the job before Mom kicked him out). Stephen lived with his wife-to-be, Nancy, and worked as a trader at the Philadelphia Stock Market. Gordon was in school in Vermont on an athletic scholarship.

By that time, all our friends knew we rescued animals, and I got a call from the next county over, asking Mom and me to take in two neglected potbellied pigs. She agreed without hesitation, and I asked my boyfriend, Woody, if we could borrow his truck.

Woody was a real car nut, with a touch of Felix Unger fastidiousness. It drove him batty to see dust on the dashboard or a gum wrapper on the floor. In parking lots, he parked way out on the edges to avoid dents and dings. The last thing he wanted was to haul a pair of dirty pigs. And though he wouldn't let me borrow the truck, very reluctantly he agreed to drive.

Mom and I constructed a makeshift crate out of pallets to hold the porkers, then we all piled in for the drive to Cape May County.

The situation was worse than we expected. The poor animals were buried up to their necks in mud and feces, so deep they could scarcely move. There was no delicate way to do this; Mom and I would have to wade into two feet of stinking crap, then physically wrestle out those filthy pigs and somehow shove them into the crate.

Holding our noses, we entered the pen, stepping into knee-high manure. Our boots made an awful sucking sound, and we instantly started slipping and sliding. The pigs, which had been immobilized a moment earlier, got very mobile very fast. They frantically sploshed around the pen, trying to evade our grasp. Soon Mom and I were covered almost head to toe in pig shit.

I tried not to look at Mom. If she cracked even a hint of a smile, I knew I would lose it. But, of course, that's exactly what happened. I caught her eye, she smirked, and soon we were laughing hysterically to the point I couldn't breathe. Mom tried to jump the larger pig, and laughed so hard she actually peed herself. My stomach was so clenched from laughing that it hurt, and I almost peed myself, too. Poor Woody looked on in disgust and horror, which made it even funnier.

She called out, "Don't worry, Wood! I promise, I'll strip off my pants and long johns and sit on my shirt, okay?"

My boyfriend raised his eyes to heaven as if to ask, "Why me?"

He got annoyed and grabbed an industrial-size aluminum trash can, scooped up the pigs one by one, and deposited them in the crate on his cargo bed.

Woody was done. "All right!" he screamed. "Get in this goddamned truck and let's go!"

As soon as we got out on the highway, it became clear that we had picked up a male and female and apparently, they were very excited about being rescued! At the sound of squealing, I turned around to see them humping like crazy, in full view of other motorists.

To understand why this was such a spectacle, you have to know a little about a pig's anatomy. Boars have corkscrew-shaped penises that can extend up to eighteen inches. Their orgasms also last a long time—up to half an hour—and they ejaculate the whole time. This wasn't just a couple of horny farm animals at play. This was the greatest show on earth.

A carload of guys caught the action and started fist-pumping and cheering. A mom in a van sped past us, I guess to keep her kids from learning too much too soon. At the sight of this freeway fornication, a couple of other drivers almost veered off the highway.

We got home, and as Mom hosed down Woody's truck, he cornered me, stuck his finger in my face, and said grimly, "Do *not* tell anybody about this."

Fast-forward to a New Year's Eve party. Warmed by a little holiday cheer, I let the story slip and soon everyone was jeering at Woody about his traveling pig sex show. End of romance.

Like clockwork, about four months later, our new sow gave birth to six baby piglets.

12

Crossroads

Once we were back home, in spite of that alarming scene in the islands, I had to badger my mother to see a doctor. She hemmed and hawed. She "forgot" to make the call. She hadn't had a personal physician in ages, so she had to track down a GP. She manufactured excuses. She wasted time.

She was frightened.

It must have been twenty years since she'd seen a doctor. In all that time, she hadn't had a mammogram, a Pap test, or even a flu shot. As a poor woman, Mom had come to view routine health care as a luxury. Something for the privileged.

But this time, I wasn't about to let up. "Woman, are you *certifiable*? Get this handled, get it treated, get it over with. Then we can all relax." I recruited my siblings, who got after her, too. Finally, reluctantly, she made the appointment.

Then came the tests, and with each one, we expected the all-clear, the clean bill of health that would let us file away this scary interlude, breathe a sigh of relief, and get back to our everyday lives. She had female problems. She could take a pill. Get a D&C. Get some rest. And get over it.

But each test led to another test, and we grew more and more anxious. First came the Pap smear, which Mom had really dreaded, which every woman dreads. It indicated an "irregularity," which meant she would need a more thorough internal exam. That exam, in turn, indicated a "suspicious area" or mass, which meant she would have to get a biopsy.

Biopsy. Oh, how my heart dropped when I heard that word. They were thinking cancer.

Characteristically, Mom made light of the situation. "There's no way I can have cancer. I was married to cancer, and we got a divorce. I've got the papers to prove it."

I wasn't nearly as confident. I wasn't confident at all. I had seen the way she'd bled.

But, hey, if Mom insisted on keeping her feelings buttoned up tight, I'd do the same, and keep her company in the wonderful world of denial. She never let me go with her to the doctor, and shared precious few details when she got back home. When I ventured to ask about it, she stonewalled. If she was unconcerned, that gave me permission to be unconcerned.

Still, it was a special kind of hell—the waiting. I tried to put it out of my mind, but it was always there, on the edge of my awareness. A specter.

To cope, I stayed hyper-busy, nose to the grindstone. It wasn't that hard. I had my company. I had clients and government officials to meet, deadlines to reach, and a staff to manage. Whenever an unwelcome thought arose—biopsy!—I pushed it out of my mind, like a bill I couldn't afford to pay. But in unguarded moments, the fear would pounce, like a monster jumping out from the shadows.

And when it did, I reminded myself that she was a farm girl. Strong as a horse. Just as healthy.

* * *

Late one afternoon, she came into the house, quietly hung up her coat, and called me into the living room. I found her perched on the edge of the sofa, pale and shaken but calm.

"So I've been to the doctor."

In that instant, I knew what was coming next.

"Before you start freaking out, Laurie, don't start freaking out. I have cancer."

I reached out for her. "Oh no. Oh no, Mom . . ."

She held up her hands, as if to ward me off. "Okay, none of that. It's cervical cancer, and it's no fun, but it's not that serious, either. They have all these good treatments nowadays. I'm going to be fine, just you wait and see."

She called my sister and brothers and said as much to them, and we believed her, first because we wanted to, and second, because she was a force of nature. We'd watched her withstand years of crushing poverty and harassment without losing her essential optimism, at least not for long. Her philosophy was: Cry your tears, then dry your tears. She was buoyant by nature, and always bounced back, as good as ever.

Besides, hadn't she suffered enough? If there's such a thing as a karmic bank account, Anne McNulty had no outstanding debts. Surely at this time in her life, she deserved nothing but sunshine and rainbows, if only to balance out all the crap my father had put her through.

Mom downplayed her condition so convincingly that, after the initial shock, I started to relax a bit. I think my siblings did, too. But we weren't in contact with her oncologist. We couldn't have dreamed that this time, our mother, that most truthful of women, was a liar.

In the early stages, cervical cancer causes no pain or other symptoms. She must have had it for a long time, and by the time she went to the doctor, it had reached stage IV. Too late for surgical intervention. Too late to save her life. Too late even to buy a lot of time.

She told no one what she already knew, that the oncologist had given her six months to live. From October to April—one more Thanksgiving, one more Christmas and New Year, and one more St. Patrick's Day.

The doctors predicted that by springtime, it would all be over.

It must have been a knockout blow, and I can only speculate why she chose to deal with it alone. Maybe she thought if she said the word out loud—"terminal"—it would be more real, and the sands in the hourglass would run down even faster. Maybe she needed to come to grips with it privately before she let on. And I'm sure she wanted to spare her family the pain.

What tipped me off, more than anything else, was her sudden emotional availability. For some people, terms of endearment come easily—the words trip over each other at each homecoming and every leave-taking. Not Mom. When we were growing up, she was the master of the four-second hug: we could embrace her for only so long before she delivered a quick peck on the cheek or forehead and gently but firmly pushed us away. For some reason, after my dad's betrayal, she had become uncomfortable with too much touching.

But following her diagnosis, she invited that physical contact. She welcomed it. She even initiated it, going in for the big hug, and then letting the hug linger.

She said the big words, too: "I love you."

"I'm proud of you."

"I'm so glad that you're my daughter."

"I'm so grateful that you're my son."

Now when Stephen came to visit, she would curl into him like a cat, rest her head in his lap and drift off to sleep, simply reveling in the closeness. It was so unlike her. The huggy-kissy quality she had lost was suddenly back.

I noticed it. It made me glad. It made me so fearful.

Reality began to set in for all of us with the start of Mom's treatment. First, her doctors said, she would have to undergo a course of chemotherapy to keep the cancer from spreading. Then she would have radiation therapy, which hopefully would destroy the existing cancer cells. We were warned it would be tough, and boy, they weren't kidding. That one-two punch turned her body into a war zone.

I don't know which treatment was worse. For starters, she had to have a port surgically implanted under her collarbone to deliver the chemotherapy medications—they called it a "cocktail," of all things—a slow drip of toxins meant to kill the cancer without killing the patient. Each infusion lasted for hours, terrible hours after which she was nauseated for days. The treatment left her with a metallic taste in her mouth, along with mouth sores that made eating almost impossible. The weight melted off her.

"On the bright side, I did gain a few pounds in the islands," she said. "So I can afford to lose a little."

And lose it she did. When we got home on treatment days, she'd disappear into the bathroom for hours, and I would hear the sound of her vomiting. Later on, I'd tap softly on the door, then slide it open to find her still there, half-lying on the floor, draped over the toilet, just trying to cool her forehead on the seat. In no time, she went from buxom and shapely to almost angular, as if she were constructed of coat hangers.

I tried to entice her with simple foods, things she liked, like vanilla ice cream or yogurt or her favorite Philly soft pretzels. She still loved pizza, but couldn't even open the box without sighing, knowing she probably wouldn't be able to keep it down.

"It's come to this," she said with resignation. "Pizza-phobia."

I was told to wear rubber gloves to wash her clothes and bedding and stash throwaway items in two plastic bags before dumping them. After chemo sessions, we were told, the toxic drugs could linger for up to two days in her urine, in her vomit, and even in her tears. Mom found grim humor in all of this, and described herself as "a walking Love Canal."

Radiation, if possible, was even tougher, especially at the beginning, when the side effects hit like a sledgehammer. To prepare for the treatment, Mom would lie on a gurney and be surrounded with "immobilization devices" to keep her body still for the procedure. The technician would slide her into a capsule-shaped machine, like an astronaut preparing for liftoff. Then this big, noisy, flashing, beeping machine would shoot beams of radiation at her body from various angles.

The treatment itself was brief, no more than ten or fifteen minutes once it started. But it came with awful side effects: crushing fatigue, diarrhea, incontinence, and the famous radiation "sunburn," the mottled reddening of the skin exposed to the radiation beams.

I understand that the treatments for some cancers are easier to take these days. I hope that's true. In Mom's day, it was like a slugfest with Mike Tyson. For a week or two, she'd go in for chemo, and then be off for a few weeks.

As lousy as the "on" weeks were, the "off" weeks really weren't much better. Just as she started to perk up, she would have to go back in for another round. Each time we headed north to the hospital, she'd start feeling sick, so apprehensive her fingers would begin to shake an hour before we even got there. Even as she kept up her happy chatter, she would lace her hands together in her lap, white-knuckling, a small gesture that broke my heart.

Luckily, as my own boss, I could adjust my schedule and set up my mobile office right there in the room at Cooper University Hospital in Camden. For me, this was a crash course: Cancer 101. Soon I thought of myself as the chemo queen, a lay expert in the treatment process and its wide-ranging after-effects.

But whenever I'm tempted to feel proud of my helpfulness, all I have to do is think of the time I forgot to take her to a chemo appointment. I don't know, I just blanked on it—or maybe I blocked it out. My poor mom stood dressed and waiting at the door, ready to go for her cancer treatment, and her devoted daughter didn't show. It fills me with remorse, even today.

In her lowest moments, Mom reminded me that if this was what it took to make her well, then we'd just have to suck it up. She needed to believe she'd get better. She refused to consider any other possibility.

God knows she kept her chin up, but at times, her very spunkiness took a toll on me. I got impatient with her, and critical. Why couldn't she just let loose, cry, rage, curse, or shake her fist at the heavens? I sure did.

But she insisted on being the good sport—"making cancer fun," as she called it. Worse, she apologized to me because, as the only one at home, I had become her unofficial caretaker. She didn't want to be a burden.

"Mom," I said, "*please* don't feel that way, because I don't."

Soon after her diagnosis, she had to stop working, but thanks to her insurance—the fabulous union insurance she'd never used when she was healthy—most of her medical bills were paid. It was a blessing. It was one less thing to worry about.

Her teamster buddies and other friends were sweet and supportive, bombarding her with flowers, gifts, and candy. Every day, the mailbox overflowed with get-well cards. One of her favorites featured a cartoonish hillbilly draining a jug of moonshine, surrounded by a pig and a dog and a bunch of chickens. On the front it said: "We heard yore feeling poorly. Git well soon!"

Hokey as hell. Just perfect for the Funny Farmer.

She pressed each of the cards into the pages of her scrapbook. And she answered them all.

Even in her weakened state, she kept up the farm, pitching hay and mucking out pens. Most of all, she took comfort in the animals. On pleasant days, she'd sit outside on her favorite carved pine bench, relaxing under the trees, surrounded by goats and pigs and relishing their company.

"It's good," she said. "It's so peaceful."

For all the physical discomfort associated with her treatments, it was especially harrowing for Mom to lose her lustrous golden-brown curls. Though she had been warned to expect it, it still jolted her to brush her hair and pull away a handful of hair, or to find clumps of it on her pillow in the morning. Worse yet was when her eyelashes and eyebrows fell out. Without them, her face looked vacant, featureless, like one of those Styrofoam wig heads. She was certainly just as pale.

Finally, rather than deal with the endless molting, she had me cut her remaining hair short, and then I shaved it all off. The wigs were my gift to her; I must have bought ten styles, in her natural color as well as the platinum shades she used to love. Every morning, before putting on the hairpiece du jour, she would pencil in her eyebrows and apply some lipstick and blush.

"Never leave the house without a little makeup," she said. "When you look good, you feel good."

Months went by with no discernible improvement in her condition. We soldiered on, recognizing that we were in this for the long haul. And unbelievably, at a certain point, cancer became background, as poverty had been so many years earlier. This was our lot, our reality. The radiation, the chemo, and all the rest were dirty jobs that had to be done, day by day, week after week, to help her survive. All of us—Cathy, Stephen, Gordon, and I—believed she would, because she was indestructible, after all, she was our mom.

It's not that she was a good patient—she was an impatient patient, she disliked being sick. But in spite of her prognosis, in defiance of it, Mom refused to die. That woman dug in her heels and insisted on living: Six months. Twelve months. Eighteen months. Two years. And more. Stubbornly, she continued to outlast the doctor's expectations. She faced cancer as she had faced every rough patch. She took it on and gave it hell. That's who she was.

"When I'm ready to die, I'll let you know," she said. "Until then, don't start counting my money."

=========== Animal Tails ===========

Jelly in the Pit

When I first looked at the Mizpah farm, one of the biggest selling points (besides the acreage, pastures, and barn) was the garage, which had its own pit. I'm a gearhead at heart, having learned from Barney and a pile of Chilton manuals how to do everything from change the oil to fix a carburetor to tear down, rebuild, and replace a transmission.

As a girl, I was known for buying a couple of hoopties, stripping the parts from one, popping them in the other, and, most of the time, ending up with a pretty decent vehicle. One time, when my accelerator cable broke in transit, I fixed it with a tampon string. Like Barney, I always had cool classic convertibles, temperamental European models that constantly needed repair. With a garage pit, I thought, I could wrench my own cars and save a heap of money.

Unfortunately, the pit didn't last. One day when I came in from work, I heard distressed whinnying somewhere near the farmhouse. I poked around the yard and woods, trying in vain to find the source. It took a quick head count of the horses to know that Jelly was missing.

I searched all around the farm, calling her name. Well, you guessed it—when I walked past the garage, the door was open, and I was horrified to see that this 1,200-pound mare had somehow fallen into the pit. Normally, a horse would never walk into a garage with all of those foreign objects and tools. I never suspected or imagined that this is where she could be. I always laid a plank crosswise over the pit to keep anyone from accidentally falling in. But Jelly walked into the garage and stepped on the plank, which gave way under her weight.

The pit was the size and dimensions of a grave: about ten feet long, eight feet deep and four feet wide. It just fit poor Jelly, who couldn't go back or forth more than a foot. The first thing I did was squeeze down into the space alongside her and check her for injuries. It was a relief to find that she was okay. She nickered softly and nudged my shoulder, happy to be found, but I was already on the verge of tears. How on earth was I going to get her out of there?

I thought about bringing in a forklift, hoping I could get a sling under her belly and lift her out that way. But the ceiling was too low for the lift. On to Plan B. I decided I would toss in three bales of hay, hoping Jelly would just walk out like they were steps.

Instead, she just stood there and ate the hay like it was a buffet. By nightfall, Jelly seemed calm, so I lowered her down a bucket of water. I had no choice but to sleep on it and figure it out in the morning.

In the morning after feeding, I came up with plan C: I would fill the pit with water and just "float" her out! Brilliant! But that didn't work, either—Jelly floated a bit, but that didn't mean she could scramble out of that damned deep ditch. Finally Plan D was successful. It consisted of filling the pit with sand.

Yes, it was a solution, but nothing about it was simple. It took hours and hours of pouring fresh sand into the pit, then jumping back in and packing it down, lifting Jelly's front feet to make sure it didn't turn into quicksand around her ankles, then adding some more. Then I would do the same to her back feet. It operated like locks in a canal. Lifting her front, then her back, and repeating the same process over and over. Gradually, the sand pile got so high that it was easy for Jelly to step out. She shook off sand and ran from the garage, relieved and happy to be free. Her only injury was a scrape on her ankle.

I'm so lucky that Jelly's the one who fell in, and not one of my crazy boys, like her boyfriend, Politico. I would never have been able to work in the pit alongside an unpredictable horse like him, and he truly might have died there. I knew that Jelly, on the other hand, wouldn't try to kick or hurt me. She was remarkably patient during the eight to ten hours I spent trying to get her out.

I was so happy that Jelly was alive and well. But sadly, it was the end of my fun as a grease monkey. The following week, I filled in the pit, cemented it over, and found an outside mechanic.

13

Nightfall

Anyone who's seen someone through a serious illness knows how grueling it can be. The roller coaster of hope and hopelessness. The inability to help in a way that actually changes things. When my mother was sick, I felt uniquely, maddeningly powerless. I can't count the times I wanted to just run away.

For me, the nights were hardest. There was something scary about sundown, as if the shadows were a kind of omen. Sometimes when I got up from bed to check on Mom—she still slept on that broken-down pullout couch—I thought I could hear her whimpering in her sleep.

Daytimes, by contrast, were almost normal. We continued to do fun stuff, scheduling our outings between treatment weeks, when Mom was more likely to feel okay. She would get all dolled up, draw on her face, put on one of those blonde wigs, and we'd be off. We went to the movies and to concerts. We saw Richard Chamberlain as Henry Higgins in a production of *My Fair Lady* in Philadelphia. As usual, Mom saved the programs and the ticket stubs and entered them in her scrapbook. By then, her stack of scrapbooks numbered a couple of dozen; stacked on top of each other, they would have almost scraped the ceiling.

She was determinedly upbeat, but looked like a woman with cancer, so thin and frail. Her clothes hung on her, and when she undressed, every rib stuck out, along with all the knobs of bones along her spine. Thank God she was receptive to hugs. While I didn't squeeze too hard—she seemed almost breakable—I didn't want to ever let go.

Things took a turn for the worse one Sunday morning. It began like any other. After feeding the animals, we were relaxing with coffee and the Sunday paper and the TV news. I started noodling around at the upright piano, trying to pick out an old show tune. When I forgot the next chord, I called to Mom, who slid in next to me on the bench, lifted her hands, and pounded out a discordant noise that was anything but musical.

"Mom, will you quit screwing around? Just show me."

She blinked at the keyboard, then banged her hands down again. More of the same tuneless racket.

She started to laugh, and I rolled my eyes. Always the jokester. "Show me the damned chord, please."

When her hands hit the keys for the third time, I realized that this was no joke. For some reason, my mother, for whom music came as naturally as breathing, was unable to play the piano.

Later on, when she was out of earshot, I called her chemotherapy nurse, Chrissy, who had become a good friend, and explained what had happened.

"What do you think it is? A side effect of the chemo?"

Chrissy listened in silence. Then in an urgent voice she said, "Laurie, get her to the hospital. Make an appointment now. *Go.*"

An MRI revealed that Mom's cancer had metastasized, spreading to her lungs, lymph nodes, and brain. A tumor pressing on part of her brain had affected her coordination, which explained the piano incident. In a matter of days, she would be struggling to speak and write.

Her cancer was out of control, like a wildfire.

It was a shattering development and a slap in the face of our smiley-face optimism. More and more, I caught a glimpse of what could lie ahead. Maybe she wasn't going to get better, after all.

The woman looked as if she'd just been torn from the pages of *Vogue*, a tall brunette in a white lab coat with a clipboard under her arm and heels that made a brisk click on the hallway floor.

Distractingly beautiful, with huge brown eyes and an airbrushed complexion, she looked more like a TV doctor than the real thing. But she was for real, all right—this was Mom's neurosurgeon.

"Won't you come with me," she said, less a question than an order. We went into a small glassed-in conference area down the hall from Mom's hospital room and faced each other across a glossy table. The neurosurgeon explained that the planned operation, called a craniotomy, would mean boring a hole in my mother's skull to help relieve the pressure on her brain. In all likelihood, it would restore her ability to speak, and rather quickly as well.

"For real?" I exclaimed. "Thank you! It's the first good news I've heard in months." I went right to hopefulness, or as it's known in my family, self-delusion.

The doctor quickly set me straight. "Please don't misunderstand, Laurie," she said, looking beautiful and sympathetic. "This really is a stopgap measure. I wouldn't think of it as anything approaching a long-term solution."

She let that sink in for a beat, then added, "There is a benefit, in that the procedure will enable your mother to speak again, and that's very important right now. It will give her time to say her goodbyes. Get her affairs in order."

Gut punch.

For some reason, I felt up in arms, even combative. "Get her affairs in order?" I scoffed. "What's that mean? Time to divvy up the family silver? Settle the compound in Hyannisport? My mother has nothing."

The doctor wasn't offended; if anything, she was even gentler with me. "Well," she said, patting my hand, "the procedure will help."

Back in the 1960s, in her landmark book *On Death and Dying*, psychiatrist Elisabeth Kübler-Ross identified five stages of grief, starting with denial, and followed by anger, bargaining, depression, and acceptance.

Early on our family got stuck in denial, and that's where we planted our flag. It felt safe there. Denial was like a protective cocoon. It let us believe that our mother, though sick now, would be better soon.

Now we understood it was time to speed through the rest of those grief stages, like cramming for a very final exam.

I had denial down pat, I'd been in denial since her diagnosis, three years earlier. My next stop was the anger booth. Most often, cervical cancer is caused by the human papillomavirus (HPV), a sexually transmitted infection, and I had to wonder if my Casanova of a father had brought something home that would later cause Mom's cancer.

For a bitter moment, I was also angry at Mom, furious, beside myself. She had never taken care of herself, even after she had insurance. Because of that, all of this.

Along with all this chaos came depression, this low-grade misery. There were times I closed the door to my office, fell to my knees, and just lost it.

Please don't hurt my mom.

That last stage—acceptance—was elusive. I swear to God, I don't know if we ever got close to it. For Mom's part, that bullheaded Irishwoman never acknowledged the gravity of her condition.

I didn't sidestep the bargaining stage, either. It was late in the day to start cutting deals, but I hadn't kept my girlhood vow—to buy a farm, a place where Mom could retire and rescue animals full-time. She still believed in the promise, the someday we'd talked about all our lives, and had a childlike faith that it would happen. And though I had been looking around for the right property since she became sick, the one deal I had pursued had fallen through. Time was growing short.

Maybe if I kept my promise, God would let me keep my mother, too.

"When I'm ready to die, I'll let you know," she said if anyone broached the subject. Then came the punchline: "Until then, don't start counting my money."

About ten days later, Cathy, Stephen, and I hunkered down in the hospital waiting room, sitting on hard plastic molded chairs, chugging cafeteria coffee, and reading outdated copies of *Reader's Digest*, *Time*, and *Cosmopolitan*. They must have seen me coming, because there was even a dog-eared copy of *Flying* magazine. I got through a mountain of magazines during the surgery, which lasted five hours, from ten in the morning till three in the afternoon.

In the recovery room, Mom was hooked to more tubes and wires than a marionette. Under a turban of white bandages, she looked up at her assembled children and managed a groggy smile.

The post-op checklist was a long one. She would have to relearn to stand, walk and talk. She would have to relearn all the "activities of daily living" like dressing, using the phone, taking her own meds, and, heaven help us, "toileting." We should expect all her emotions to come into play—anger and frustration and sadness and more frustration. We shouldn't be surprised if she lashed out, even at us, and mostly at us, because we would be there. Before her discharge, we met with a trio of therapists who mapped out a rehab plan. Each one warned us to expect a long, slow road back.

"Swelling in the brain is expected after surgery," said the physical therapist, "so recovery will take time, and the benefits won't be immediate."

"Don't talk down to her or use baby talk," said the speech therapist. "Speak clearly, and be willing to repeat yourself. Be patient with her as she tries to reply. If she can't understand you, don't shout. She's not deaf."

"The simplest activities will confound her, like buttoning a shirt or correctly holding a fork," said the occupational therapist. "Respect her limits, and be proud of her accomplishments."

Once she was back on her feet, we were told, she would want to walk for exercise, but she should avoid heavy lifting and other strenuous activities.

"I guess that means no pig wrestling," I said. The therapists smiled, with no idea that I was serious.

As we left the hospital, a friendly patient advocate reminded me that there were all kinds of support groups available to people like us, family members as well as patients; would I like some names and numbers?

"Thanks, anyway," I said. "We're kind of in the suck-it-up school of cancer. If I change my mind, I promise you'll hear me screaming."

In our family, I had always been the crybaby, the weeping willow, and my sister the no-nonsense taskmaster. With our mother's illness, it was like we switched personalities—just as

Mom and I had in that *Freaky Friday* episode in the Caribbean. All of a sudden, I was the drill sergeant, doling out orders and tough love: "Time for your walk, Mom. Come on now, no bullshit, no excuses!" Poor Cathy had a hard time looking at Mom without bursting out in tears.

As promised, her speech returned, and very quickly. One day she put on an old souvenir T-shirt we had given her as kids that read, HELP, I'M TALKING AND I CAN'T SHUT UP.

In the months following the operation, it truly was back to basics—as basic as the ABCs. In addition to everything else on her to-do list, Mom had to teach herself to write again. I would often come home to find her bent over a copybook, carefully tracing out the letters of her name like an earnest kindergartener.

For all she'd endured, she laughed a lot, even at her illness—especially at her illness, as if she could kid her cancer into remission. Whatever kept her going at that point, audacity or plain old stubbornness, it must have been working, at least up to a point. Four years ago, the doctors had given her six months to live. She was still here, still planning for the future, still smiling.

As a family, we agreed that it was time to discontinue chemotherapy and radiation, and almost immediately we recognized it as the right decision. Without the constant onslaught of treatments, Mom perked up like a flower. For her, just to feel not sick was to feel wonderful. She was so glad to be done with those long, white-knuckle drives to the hospital. Her hair began to grow in and covered the Frankenstein stitches crisscrossing her skull.

I remembered the beautiful doctor and all she had said about last goodbyes and loose ends and stopgap measures.

Don't count out my mom, I thought. *She's mighty like an oak.* Remarkably, miraculously, she rallied again.

Animal Tails

Jethro and Lorenzo

Donkeys form strong pair bonds. When those bonds are broken by death or separation, donkeys grieve as long and hard as some people do. They become depressed, and may even fall sick or die. Jethro the donkey was best friends for years with a horse called Smokey.

When Smokey died, Jethro was so sad. My heart went out to him, and I made it my mission to find him another friend. But animal friendships, like those between humans, can't be forced. Introducing the wrong animal can awaken a donkey's territorial instinct, which can lead to fighting.

With careful supervision, I brought a new horse to Jethro's pasture. The two tolerated each other, but Jethro kept to himself, and the attempted match was a dud. Ditto with one of our other donkeys.

Then along came redemption in the form of a llama named Lorenzo. Lorenzo once was owned by farmers in Vineland. When the couple moved into a senior community, they left the llama alone on their property, and stopped by only occasionally to feed him. He was very lonely.

Months passed, and Animal Control got complaints from neighbors who said the llama had been abandoned. An investigator went out to the old farm, and found Lorenzo had nothing to eat but hay that had already gone moldy. He asked the farmers for permission to bring Lorenzo to the Funny Farm. I had previously found homes for their mules, Liberty and Free, and they gratefully accepted.

Lorenzo was just the medicine Jethro needed, and I didn't need to match them up, because they found each other. It's possible that Jethro was attracted by Lorenzo's coloring. The llama has brown and white patches that are very similar to Smokey's. Whatever the attraction, the two animals bonded and soon were inseparable. Lorenzo helped Jethro come back to life. He began eating again and became the roly-poly animal he had once been. Jethro helped to resocialize Lorenzo, who had lived alone in that field for so long, he was shy around humans. I wouldn't say he loves people—yet—but he sure loves Jethro. He also loves bananas. And if you offer him one, he'll gladly kiss you on the lips.

Sometimes, the best medicine is to just let nature take its course. This is one of the strongest and most unlikely friendships around the farm. Older donkeys get fat pockets on their butts that look like Kardashian ass implants. During a recent outdoor wedding, Jethro the donkey stuck his keister through the fence to scratch an apparent itch and it looked like he did an entire dance while the wedding party was looking on. The bride was not amused.

14

Homeward Bound

"Fasten your seat belt, Mom. Here's where the road gets rocky."
Hanging a right off the Black Horse Pike, we plunged into a maze of back-country roads. The convertible top was down. The classic rock was up and blasting. My mother had to hold on to her Art-Z Graphics ball cap as we hurtled into the secluded heart of the New Jersey Pinelands.

"Hey, mind slowing it down a little bit?" she shouted. "I might like to see the scenery."

"We've been waiting long enough," I shouted in return. "I want to *get there*." I hit the accelerator until every pebble in the road lifted us off our seats.

Besides trees, there wasn't a whole lot to see in this part of South Jersey anyway: a couple of taxidermists' shops, a gun club, a last-chance diner, and a park with benches, all in a labyrinth of pitch pines and scrub pines so thick they almost blotted out the sunlight.

In the midst of all this nowhere was our someday: a fifteen-acre farm with a shabby house, a big old barn, and a couple of sheds, ringed by fields of more pines.

Well, it wasn't quite ours, yet. I had submitted my offer of the full asking price in the hopes of a speedy purchase. I was optimistic because Mizpah wasn't exactly the Main Line, and most people weren't interested in migrating into the deep woods. But I wasn't the only interested party. My real estate agent, a friend named Jen, said another buyer had already outbid me and looked ready to get aggressive about it.

I wasn't giving up. Maybe it was magical thinking—okay, clearly it was magical thinking, wishing on a star, bargaining with God—but I figured if I did a good thing, maybe it would cancel out a bad thing. By getting the farm for my mother, I reasoned, surely she would get the chance to live in it.

The country cousin of nearby Mays Landing, Mizpah once was a factory town, a hub of garment-making and the center of South Jersey's Jewish community. By the late 1990s, the factories were long gone and a former rail line had been abandoned. As far as I could tell, by the year 2000 Mizpah was mostly hicks and sticks. But that was fine by me. As one of the former who comes from the latter, I considered both terms to be compliments. I would be right at home, and so would my mother.

"Now we'll be real Pineys," I told Mom. "We'll have to get the bumper sticker."

She smiled in the seat next to me. Her once-pretty features were pinched and sharp, and her skin almost paper-white. She was still too thin. But her golden-brown hair was back, abundant and soft, like duck down. Best of all, she was feeling marvelous.

After the brain surgery, and especially after we suspended those draining medical treatments, she had come back to life, like a wilting flower that miraculously springs up with a little water and sunshine. She began to eat heartily—lots of takeout pizza—and spent more time outdoors, keeping up the farm and all the animals with her old vigor. She laughed. She made plans. It was almost four years since the original diagnosis, in which she had been given six months to live.

That was my mom. Always outfoxing them.

We turned onto Railroad Boulevard, a narrow two-lane road that threads through the pine forest. It led us into even deeper woods, and I had to swerve to avoid the herds of deer and flocks of wild turkeys that occasionally picked their way along the roadside. At first, I sped right past the entrance to the farm, which was completely hidden from the road. Then we doubled back, and drove through a split rail fence and onto the grounds.

We jerked to a stop.

I turned to look at Mom.

Mom looked all around.

This was the moment I had imagined most of my life. Our someday, and the fulfillment of that long-ago promise.

At first, her expression was inscrutable. She said nothing, but slowly climbed out of the car, took a deep breath, and trudged down the dirt pathway that curved by the house and barn and pastures.

Suddenly the farm's many flaws stuck out, as if they were marked by neon arrows: the house's peeling paint and wobbly porch rails, the mossy greenish mold crawling along the stone foundation, the buckled pasture fences, the sea of overgrown weeds and grass.

I began talking at her like a used-car dealer trying to close a sale. "Yeah, I know it needs a little work, but it's mostly cosmetic, don't you think? And, hey, even the barn is better than the house we're living in now. And look at how much land! Fifteen acres, Mom. It's like the Ponderosa!"

Still she was silent. Was she disappointed? Was the place too shabby? She didn't hate it, did she?

She kept trudging along, hands thrust into her pockets, surveying the landscape.

"Job one: paint the barn red!" I said. "Because who in hell has a blue barn? Then we'll fix it up just the way you like it. And, boy, you can have lots more animals. All the animals in the world."

Tiring a bit, she leaned against a pasture fence, and I swore I saw a flush of pink in those pale features.

She turned to me. "It's perfect." She ambled on down the pathway, a lady of the manor in cowgirl boots and jeans.

There would be lots of work to do. The farmhouse was a wreck inside and needed a total overhaul. The previous residents had been heavy smokers, and the once-white walls were stained yellow from nicotine. Their dog had gnawed big holes in the doors and doorjambs and left urine stains on the floor. The bathroom was a wreck. The pool out back, filled with water as black as India ink, for some reason had become a repository for athletic equipment: baseball bats, Wiffle balls, golf clubs, hockey sticks.

The artist in me took issue with the lacquered golden oak kitchen cabinets and the stone countertops, which were silverish with a weird lavender cast.

But in the end, the many drawbacks didn't matter. We had land fever. It really was the land, not the house, that sold us. Living here, we would have enough space for hundreds of animals.

The bidding war on the property went on for months—interminable, teeth-gnashing months. I met the owners of the farm, and when I explained what Mom hoped to do there, establish an animal rescue, they seemed delighted. But every time the place seemed within our grasp, the other bidder upped his offer, the owner hesitated, and the stalemate continued.

I was about to go to the Bank for a loan when Cathy stepped up. She, too, wanted Mom's dream to come true, and offered to kick in her own spare cash. Pooling our resources, we were able to offer one hundred and seventy thousand dollars for the farm. But our joy was short-lived. About thirty-six hours later, our rival bidder inched ahead to a hundred eighty. Ouch.

Again I considered going to the Bank, but I would be taking on more debt than I could manage. The cupboard was bare. I was tapped out, finished, kaput. With no point in pursuing it, reluctantly I wrote off the whole deal.

Not so my mother. She went out and bought dishware to go with those lavender counters, eight glass place settings in a lurid eggplant purple. I guess the stress of it all—her illness dragging out, the farm deal dragging out—was getting to me, because when I came upon her unpacking the dishes, I lost it.

"Mom, can you get it through your head that we've been outbid by ten thousand bucks? We're not even in the ballpark. And you go and buy those ugly dishes. Purple!"

She was in one of her annoyingly sunny moods. "Now don't give up the ship quite yet, Laurie. I have a good feeling about that place. It just felt homelike to me." She replaced the top dish in its box and folded the box closed. "Let's not unpack these until we get to the farm."

"Now hear this," I said. "This place is out of our reach. Maybe we can start over, find another one. And maybe we should forget the whole damned thing. I'm sick of it."

"Laurie, would you calm down, please? It's not over till it's over."

It was foolish to get upset but, dissecting my reaction now, I think I felt guilty because I couldn't keep my promise, and angry because of the guilt.

I also felt poor—that old, familiar, not-good-enough feeling—because I couldn't match the competing offer. And of course, feeling poor made me feel sorry for myself. Add to all that a heaping helping of regret—I had let down the person I loved most, and here she was being all adorable and optimistic about it. Yes, it was a full circle of misery, all self-inflicted.

But I was still sore about those purple plates. I wanted to smash them to smithereens. Mom got another set, festooned with roosters and barns and cute sayings: "A little dirt doesn't hurt." "I wasn't born in a barn, but I got here as fast as I could."

"Now that's more like it," I said.

At the end of June came the call we had been waiting for, from our Realtor friend Jen, who told us the property owner had accepted our bid over the other one, even though we offered less. Cathy and I were at Mom's, sorting through the clothes and crockery and books she had accumulated over twenty-eight years in that hovel. There were cardboard boxes of boots and sneakers and toys from when we were kids, and clothes with our names on the waistbands or inside back collars in black Sharpie. There were all my elementary school art supplies, and a sheaf of my early drawings: cats and cows and horses and sheep, all the Funny Farm animals.

Inside the pantry were enough expired dollar-store canned goods to survive an apocalypse. And, as always, rubber bands—drawers filled with rubber bands, bundles of them, held together by other rubber bands. It was time to get rid of it all.

"Anyway, it's all yours, lock, stock, and tumbleweeds," Jen chirped. "Now, just a little more paper shuffling and you can take possession. Congratulations, girl!"

I thanked her, hung up the phone, then turned to my sister with a bleak smile. "Well! Guess who's the owner of a great big old farm in the Pinelands?" I tipped back my head. Old trick, holds the tears in. Cathy was on me in a second, pulling me into a bear hug so tight it hurt.

"Now don't you dare," she said in a rough voice. "She got to see it. She got to dream about it. She got to buy those damned plates. It gave her hope."

Mom had died two weeks earlier.

After a cancer battle that raged on for more than four years, how could her death have been unexpected? And yet it was. She had rallied, like Lazarus, after her brain surgery, so much so that we started believing in miracles. But as sometimes happens with terminal patients, as she entered the end stage, she took an amazing turn for the better, followed by a rapid turn for the worse. Her decline, when it came, was swift. She faded before our eyes like a Polaroid in reverse.

The time was past for bargaining and denial, but even then, she fought. In the hospital, she had scrawled her initials on a do-not-resuscitate order, ensuring that if her breathing stopped or she went into a coma, there would be no heroic measures to save her. Now she demanded that we rescind it.

I'd heard that sometimes, people need permission from their loved ones to die, to go into the light, and now, clumsily, I tried to grant her that permission. "It's okay to let go, Mom, and go onto the next thing. Just think, you'll be able to see Mom-Mom and Pop-Pop and Uncle Ed and Aunt Mary. They're waiting for you."

She glared at me, furiously. "Let 'em wait," she spat out. "I'm not going anywhere."

After that, I no longer insisted to her that she was dying, did not demand that she accept her fate or make her peace. What good would it have done? She was a young woman. She loved her life. If she clung to hope, if she took comfort in denial, it would have been cruel to take these things away from her.

Cathy moved back to the farm, and a rotating team of hospice workers came by twice a week to help, making it possible for us to keep Mom comfortably at home. But even with their guidance, we were no Florence Nightingales. I'll be forever haunted by one incident when I administered more than the prescribed amount or morphine—four times the proper dose. For days, Mom tossed in her bed, delirious and sweating and muttering in the tangled sheets. She survived my inept caregiving but, in the words of her hospice nurse, "probably had some pretty trippy dreams."

In and out of a sedative fog, she once again retreated from us emotionally, warding off the hugs and kisses and hand-holding. She even spurned her dog, a white German shepherd named Baby, and pushed her off the bed when she tried to snuggle with her.

So many times, she had said, "When I'm ready to die, I'll let you know."

And she did.

On June 25, 2000, at about two in the morning, I sat straight up in bed, instantly awake from a deep slumber. Something told me to check in on Mom. Creeping into the living room, I knelt on the side of the pull-out sofa and watched as she heaved a last, deep, ragged breath. Immediately her face softened and relaxed, and she was utterly still. She was gone, one month shy of her fifty-third birthday.

I ran back to the bedroom and switched on the bedside lamp. "Cathy, wake up. I think Mom just died."

My sister blinked open her eyes and stopped me before I could return to the living room. "Don't you go back in there," she said. "If she knows you're there, she'll try to come back. Let her go easily."

So I sat up all night, knees drawn up to my chin, just listening. All I could hear was Robert Goulet, crooning on the stereo, softly, the soundtrack of her last days.

When daylight came, Cathy and I gathered ourselves, returned to the living room, and saw for sure that she was dead.

My poor little mommy, so shriveled and small, thin as Pick-Up Sticks. Her tiny hands rested gently on the quilt-top, weighing nothing at all.

Nobody would ever hurt her again.

For a while I sat by the sofa where she had slept every night, in the shabby house that she had never escaped and now never would. I thanked her for making the house a home for us kids, for Gordon, for Jimmy Bacon, and for so many homeless people and animals. I let myself cry a bit for all the things I had been unable to give her, the someday that had been just out of our reach.

All day long Cathy paced in and out. She wept and walked away, returned to look at Mom, then walked away again. Stephen came with his wife, Nancy, kissed Mom's hand, then wandered outside to lose himself in what was left of our woods. Uncle John came with his wife, Bernadette, and my cousins Nikki and Annie. And then in a few hours the funeral director came to carry the body away.

With her death, I was faced with a dilemma. City mouse or country mouse? Urban cowgirl or homesteader? Demi Moore's loft or a farm in the middle of the Pinelands? It had been my goal to buy the farm for my mother, not to live in it full-time myself, at least not for long. It wasn't too late for me to back out, was it?

I posed the question as if I had a choice, but I already knew the answer.

I was a farm owner now, if not yet a farmer. And though Mom was gone, my responsibility to her animals—and to her—was unchanged. If only for now, it was up to me to move to the new Funny Farm.

If I bailed, I knew that woman would come back to haunt me.

Animal Tails

Politico

I've set aside a special pasture at the farm for retired racehorses, far back in a field, away from our visitor area. It's called the time-out pen. Some of these horses were mistreated during their track careers by impatient trainers and jockeys. As a result, they continue to fear people and can't be trusted not to bite or kick. One of my naughtiest is a Thoroughbred named Politico.

Although Politico is lightning-fast—really a blur when he runs—he wasn't a moneymaker. To my knowledge, he never won a race. When his owner realized he wouldn't see a return on his investment, Politico was not treated well and was sent to auction. He almost certainly would have been slaughtered if not for a compassionate horse lover who rescued him and asked if we could take him at the Funny Farm.

Politico is sleek, beautiful, and obsidian black. He's also balky and short-tempered—in horsey parlance, "hot-blooded." But while Shannon could be temperamental—bucking when I tried to ride him, head-butting Stephen in the snowball incident—Politico has inflicted real injury, left me with lasting scars, and put me in the hospital twice.

One time, I was feeding Politico when he bit me, and practically took my thumb off. Apparently, he didn't think I was pouring his food in fast enough. Another time, when I opened the pasture gate, he must have thought it was post time, because he bolted, running me over. The volunteers tell me I fell flat on my back, staggered to my feet, then swooned back to my knees. I don't remember any of it. I ended up in the hospital with a concussion and short-term memory loss, but still loved him just the same. After all, it wasn't his fault he was treated so badly.

Politico has calmed down a lot over the years, in large part because of a "widowed" mare named Jelly, whose longtime mate Peanut Butter died of asthma. Though Jelly is an older woman—about twenty-seven, to Politico's twenty—they're a devoted pair. Unfortunately, Politico cannot be separated from Jelly for even a few moments without having a tantrum, and when that big boy explodes, he's fully capable of busting down stalls and people. That's why I pray that he doesn't outlive Jelly. Or hopefully, by then, he will have become a sweet old man and it won't matter.

We do have one very gentle racehorse with impressive bloodlines who was a consistent winner. Her track name was High Jingo but in 2019, when she retired to the Funny Farm, her former owners renamed her "Anna." Anna was sired by Shackleford, who placed fourth in the 2011 Kentucky Derby, won the Preakness Stakes the same year, and won more than $3 million over the course of his career. Her mother, Karakorum Karen, was a descendant of Derby winner Northern Dancer.

High Jingo herself—Anna—ran a total of fifteen races from 2016 to early 2020 and won three. Unlike some of our Thoroughbreds, she's relaxed and even-tempered, so I paired her with a gelding named Canyon, who lost his left eye tangling with a barbed wire fence. Canyon and Anna are now a team and, each morning, walk together to the farmhouse in search of peppermint treats (yes, horses love mint!).

As for Politico, though his disposition has improved over time, he may never completely recover from the trauma of his past life. He'll never fully trust people, so we can't fully trust him. That's why he'll stay in the far pasture on visiting days, in permanent time-out. Scars run deep.

PART III

Oh Give Me a Home

15

Moving Day

It didn't take more than a few days to empty out the old house. We just grabbed a bunch of oversize Hefty bags and started shoveling. After setting aside a few mementos—Mom's nine-foot stack of scrapbooks and all those photo albums, documenting every other waking moment of our lives—there was nothing worth keeping. Nobody clamored for the purple lava lamp or demanded custody of the velvet Elvis painting. No one wanted the broken-down plaid couch. Our mother had died as she'd lived, owning nothing of value. She didn't leave a will, because what for?

The only thing I asked for was that scarred upright piano, because I was the only one in the family who played much. And of course, I had agreed to take the animals—all thirty-five of them, including a dozen cats, a couple of goats, the usual assortment of chickens, roosters, ducks, geese, and pigs, a single horse, and her dog, Baby.

Closing the door for the last time was more emotional for me than I expected. The place was a dump, had always been a dump: ramshackle, godforsaken, plug-ugly. But it was also home, the place where we all had grown up, where my mother had lived for more than a quarter century, where she had died.

"When I'm gone," she always joked, "just put a match to this place."

But she had loved it, too. As she used to sing, it was her shanty in old shanty town, and she was its queen, "waiting there with a silvery crown."

But no one else had reason to love that little house in the woods. After we cleared out, it was never occupied again. The next year, a bulldozer came in and plowed the place to rubble.

To move the menagerie, I lined up a caravan of borrowed trailers and trucks and recruited my best friends Lynee and Andy and my brother and sister. Gordon had begun a life in California after college and was still 3,000 miles away. "Are you all in for this?" I said warningly. "It'll be dirty and smelly and no fun."

"How tough can it be?" asked Andy. "Just promise us some takeout pizza and a six-pack, and we're there."

Pizza and beer. Always the coin of the realm in our lives.

The hardest part was relocating the piggery, and no surprise there. Pigs are seldom cooperative and backed into a corner will throw tantrums like thousand-pound toddlers. Even the tamest of them, if displeased, are capable of charging like rhinos. And talk about strong—your average adult boar is fully capable of going nine rounds with George Foreman, then flipping George onto his own grill. The pigs bucked like broncos and squealed like Ned Beatty until we got them onto the trailer and to their new digs. But they also provided the comic relief. To watch Stephen wrassling a pig like he did as a boy was worth the price of admission. There's a reason that greased pig contests are a thing.

Once in Mizpah, I had to improvise the animals' housing, because there were no decent enclosures at the new place. One fence on the big paddock was intact, but wobbly to the point of collapse. The barn would need to be cleared out before I could use it, even on a short-term basis. So I let the goats range, and slapped together some makeshift corrals for the horse and the piggies. Luckily it was summertime, so they didn't require protection from the weather, but I'd have to get a jump on that before fall set in.

My first night there was unsettling. Eerie. After my friends waved goodbye, as I walked the beer cans and pizza boxes to the recycling bin, it struck me, full force, that my own dream—the urban-artist life—was done for, and the life I had dreamed for my mom—sung to the tune of "Old MacDonald"—now looked like my own future. I was glad no one was around. As the sun disappeared into the pines, I sagged onto the sagging porch steps, let out a despondent cry, and basically howled at the rising moon. Mom's dog Baby pushed in next to me, whimpering sympathetically.

It wasn't like me to give in to despair, and if Mom had been there she would have gotten right in my face, telling me to pull up my britches, cut the crap, and get to work. But the dream in my head, the someday I'd cherished for most of my life, had always included that crazy Irishwoman. The timing of her death two weeks before I closed on the property seemed ineffably cruel to me, a colossally unfunny cosmic joke. All that remained of her now was a small box on the purple countertop, which I would later bury on the farm grounds.

More than once, I said these things to Cathy, who reminded me that if I looked at it another way, the timing was perfect. "Mom knew we had the farm. She had that at the end, and it made her happy. But moving would have been too hard on her. She had begun the business of dying, and she had to finish it."

Nerves had something to do with my dismay, too. I was a young, single woman, all by my lonesome in the million-acre Pinelands

National Reserve, in a rural area known for pockets of drug traf-
ficking. I had heard about meth labs stuck back in those woods,
which supposedly had led to explosions and house fires.

At night, the sounds of the pine forest gave me the deep-down
willies: hooting owls, yipping foxes, and a call-and-response howl-
ing sound that could have been packs of coyotes or wolves. Inside,
I heard the relentless scurrying of rats under the front porch. My
cats would soon take care of the rat population, but that sound
was horrible, too.

But it was the sounds I couldn't identify that really made the
gooseflesh rise. The indefinable creaks and groans of the old farmhouse sounded like little monsters under the floorboards, wickedly
plotting my demise.

But the silence was the scariest of all.

I began to sleep with a baseball bat and a cast-iron frying pan,
just in case an ax murderer should come to call. Then I added to
my arsenal: my own ax, as well as Mom's rifle. I'd been a Girl
Scout, and Girl Scouts knew to be prepared.

Buyer's remorse set in. Not until I took possession of the property,
had the keys cut, and changed my mailing address did I admit
what I must have known all along, at the height of my house fever.
The new Funny Farm was a money pit. The cedar shingles fell like
rain. The paint on the porch peeled away in sheets. The foundation
was questionable. When Uncle John came down to help me install
a new pool liner, we had to put on dive gear before entering that
blackened swill.

At least a few times a day it hit me upside the head, like a brick:
*Oh my God. I emptied my bank account and borrowed from my sister
for this. Why?*

My biggest rookie mistake as a homeowner was choosing to

gut the house's one and only bathroom before I moved in, and installing a portable john outside. My second biggest mistake? Positioning the Porta Potty way across the field from the house, because I thought having it close by would be somehow indelicate.

So at night when I had to go, it meant running like Usain Bolt through pitch-dark fields, lugging my gun and cast-iron skillet, fearful that any moment I could be set upon by that ax murderer or maybe the Jersey Devil. I was always on high alert, every one of my senses tuned up. My heartbeat in my ears sounded like the theme from *Jaws*.

Until then, I had loved rip-roaring, blood-curdling horror flicks: *The Texas Chainsaw Massacre, Halloween, The Amityville Horror, Nightmare on Elm Street*. After moving to Mizpah, I never watched a scary movie again, and never put curtains on the windows, either.

If Michael Myers or Freddy Krueger was on the way, I was going to see them first.

Many times, in the months that followed, Mom would visit me in dreams. She was always smiling and rosy-cheeked, as if she had never gotten cancer, had never suffered and died. It was extraordinarily comforting, so much so that I tried to sleep longer in the morning—hard for a longtime early riser—and go to bed earlier, so we had more time together.

Cathy was upset: "Why does she visit you and not me?"

Mom made her presence known in other ways, too. They say that when someone dies, they let you know they're around by playing tricks with lights or moving household objects or sending messengers. I understand the desire to believe that finding a new penny or seeing a cardinal means a lost loved one is close by. But

I had never been the superstitious type, and I never would have bought into that craziness if I hadn't seen so much of it.

First came the light show. Inside and out, the lights flickered incessantly, so much that I called the electric company to come out and check the connection. The lineman assured me there was nothing wrong, but it continued to happen, again and again. No way was I going to be in the deep woods without lights, so I had it checked repeatedly, and was assured repeatedly that nothing was going on that would disrupt my service.

Then Mom's coffee cup—the one with "Annie" in script on the side—began to swing on its hook in the kitchen. I swear to God, once or twice it actually jumped off the hook and onto the purple counter.

I was officially spooked. The next time the outdoor lights snapped off—I was walking out to the portable toilet, of all places—I threw my arms up to heaven and yelled, "Bitch, would you cut that out? I'm fine. I love you. Just go. Don't worry about me, and stop turning off the lights. It's frickin' dark out here!"

When the lights blinked back on, I gave a laugh that sounded like a shout, and imagined I could hear her laughing in return.

Good one, Mom.

And it never happened again.

I lived at the Funny Farm for a dozen years before many people knew that I rescued animals. At work, I was still CEO Barbie, turned out for the boardroom. At home, I pulled on my Carhartt overalls and slopped hogs. Two separate worlds. That's the way I liked it.

I was secretive about the rescue stuff, for one big reason. I was concerned the farm would turn into a dumping ground for unwanted animals, and I would be overrun with pleas for help.

Young Laurie riding
her first pony.

(*below*) Annie
snuggling on the
couch with Petunia,
the house pig.

The original Funny Farm house in Turnersville getting a long-awaited new roof.

Annie McNulty's favorite thing to do was riding her horse.

Annie always found ways to take care of her animals.
Here she is trimming goat hooves herself.

(*below*) Annie's beloved first horse, Shannon O'Leary.

(*above*) Yogi the steer and his best friend, Cooper the alpaca, are inseparable.

Chickens rescued from a slaughterhouse, looking forward to a bright future at the Funny Farm.

Papa, Bo, and Luke, the three little pigs rescued from starvation.

(*below*) Emily the Emu.

Debbie De Goose.

Juliette the pig.

Stinky the skunk plays with his brothers, Chuck and Farley.

(below) Adele the diva chicken.

Jelly in the pit.

Lorenzo the llama and his best buddy,
Jethro the fifty-year-old mini donkey.

Politico the rescued racehorse.

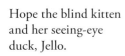

Hope the blind kitten and her seeing-eye duck, Jello.

(*above*) Steven the Canada
goose and his beloved
Angel the domestic goose.

Reggie the sheep rescued
from sacrifice.

Socks, the guardian angel of the Funny Farm.

(*below*) Aerial view of Funny Farm Rescue, as it is today.

Tucker, the megaesophagus puppy, when he first arrived at the Funny Farm.

Laurie feeding her megaesophagus dog, Chuck, in his special Bailey Chair.

At the Funny Farm, animals of different species get along. Cowboy the goat, Reggie the sheep, Yogi the steer, and Farley the dog, all have a special bond and are known as the Fabulous Four.

(*below*) Laurie has a special connection with every animal she meets.

Despite their different backgrounds, everyone is happy to be a part of the Funny Farm family.

Many odd friendships occur at the Funny Farm.

KitKat the rescued turkey.

Every animal at the
Funny Farm has their
own distinct personality.

The Funny Farm is not just a place, it's a feeling.

In a perfect world, I would have welcomed every animal in need—it's a genetic weakness, inherited from Mom—but I was just one person. My resources weren't unlimited. I think the same dilemma faces everyone who does this kind of work; there's no way to save them all. And, believe me, that is disheartening. Just try saying no when someone turns up with an animal that will certainly die if you don't lend a hand. It hurts like hell. My mother didn't have a "no" button, and I didn't, either. Over those dozen years, though few people knew I ran a rescue—unofficially— word got out that Laurie Zaleski, just like her mom, was a soft touch for homeless animals. By 2011, I had taken in more than two hundred of them. I imagined what would happen if I went public, and the thought was frightening. Anytime someone visited me or came to surrender an animal, I practically forced them to take a vow of omertà: "This is just between us, ya get it? It's our secret, ya see?"

But you know what they say: Three can keep a secret if two of them are dead.

Of course, my opposite worlds sometimes intersected. Once on the way to work I got a distress call about a baby skunk found almost drowned in someone's pool. I had no choice but to smuggle it into the office, tucked in my designer purse. Once inside, I wrapped it in a cashmere scarf and tucked it in a filing box near the baseboard heater, then quietly clued in my employees. One by one, they tiptoed in to "ooh" and "ahh" over the baby, who was unharmed and grateful to be warm and dry.

Baby skunks don't so much spray as go "poof," emitting a mild and not-terribly-pungent odor. Even so, all day long I blitzed my department with high-octane perfume—Coty's Vanilla Musk—to mask any smell. My staff cracked up when a senior manager passed through and commented on the pleasant fragrance. "How nice! Smells like springtime."

Then there was the time I took an important meeting with government officials, only to realize halfway through that I had a ginormous clod of dried horse manure stuck under my stiletto heel. For the rest of the meeting, I listened with half an ear, preoccupied with trying to pry off the clod with my other heel. Just my luck, it didn't come loose until the meeting adjourned. As the men in the room tried to wave me through the doorway—"Ladies first"—I smiled inanely and said, "Please, no! After you!"

They headed out. I scooped up the dollop of dung, shoved it in my pocket, and made my own graceful exit, waltzing like Ginger Rogers down the hall and laughing under my breath.

As the farm grew, I cleared space for pigpens and henhouses, small-animal hutches, and all manner of prefab sheds and shelters. For the goats, who loved to climb, I built a makeshift jungle gym of old ladders, picnic tables, pallets, tree stumps, and cast-off cable spools. I painted that blue barn a nice rusty red, and inside, installed a tack room and a room for hay and feed. I fenced in half a dozen fields for grazing.

Of necessity, this was done on a shoestring; I never passed a pile of discarded lumber without throwing planks onto my flatbed. But to everyone who visited, I continued to plead, "Please don't tell anyone. I can barely take care of the animals I have. I can't accept any more."

The moment of reckoning came the month my feed bill topped four thousand dollars. I knew I couldn't continue to shoulder this burden alone, and I had learned if I applied for nonprofit status—if the Funny Farm became a government-sanctioned charitable organization—not only could I hold fundraisers and accept donations, I would also get a much needed tax break on that crushing feed bill.

Seven percent of four grand was $3,360 a year. It was like one month free! Most of the other farm-related costs would be tax-exempt, too, and I could also recruit volunteers.

I still hesitated. Working for the federal government, I was well acquainted with the workings of bureaucracy, and figured starting a charity would involve mountains of paperwork. With a little research, I discovered I would have to establish a board of directors, come up with bylaws, and file articles of incorporation. I would be subject to scrutiny from federal, state, and county officials as well as the public.

But I needed help, the dollars-and-cents kind, so I decided to go for it. Altruism, idealism, love of animals—all those things aside, I just wanted a break on my damned feed bill. Anything beyond that would be gravy.

Making the decision was just the first step in a long, protracted legal slog. Obviously, I couldn't just up and declare myself the founder of a charity, therefore entitled to tax-exempt status. The state makes that decision, and the IRS has a hand in it, too. As I had expected, the paperwork was inches thick and the process tough, like a tax audit, or maybe a strip search.

The government looks for reasons to turn you down, and I was rejected a number of times for reasons I didn't fully comprehend. Over and over, I filled out those mile-long forms, trying to pinpoint where I was going wrong.

I was desperate for that tax break, and was at the end of my rope when I ended up on the phone with a state official who helped to get me over the finish line.

"I'm so confused," I said, weeping with exasperation. "I'm

trying to be more specific about my plans, I am giving you way more than you're asking for here, and still I keep getting turned down!"

In a voice like a bullhorn, she said, "That's your whole problem, dearie. Do *not* give us more than we want. Don't you add a word. That just confuses the functionaries. Get a pen and a piece of paper and write this down."

Then she explained to me, word for word, how to answer the questions that had been tripping me up. "Don't you add one more syllable! Sign it and send it!"

She was hard-boiled, sympathetic, and kind. I did as she instructed, submitted my application yet again, and crossed my fingers. It was a yearlong process.

Animal Tails

Hope and Jello

A mother cat and all but one baby were hit by a car. Some time later, a neighbor heard a frantic meow from a kitten and went to help. What he saw was a little black kitten crying next to her mother. No one heard the accident or knew how long the mom had been unable to take care of her baby, but it had been awhile. The baby was starving to death and wondered why her mom wasn't waking up to feed and take care of her. Imagine how afraid she must have been all alone in a big world.

The little black kitten was so hungry and quickly deteriorating. Her eyes were shut and she was nothing but skin and bones. The man who found her brought her to the Funny Farm after calling all the government agencies that were closed due to the Memorial Day holiday. I knew this little kitten's time was short and got right to work. Every breath seemed like her last. I kept saying, "Mama's here for you, you're going to be okay," over and over while holding her gently in my arms.

Without a second thought, I turned my kitchen sink into a trauma center, with my flashlight, Dawn dish soap, warm water, and tweezers to pick off all the fleas. The little black kitten loved her warm bath. I thought she must have fallen in a puddle of mud since her ears were filled with mud. After her bath, I wrapped her in a warm donated towel just out of the dryer and gently blew dry her long hair. She was a whole new kitten. She was beautiful.

The little black kitten drank some warm kitten formula from a syringe, but not much. She fell asleep knowing she was warm and fed and, most important, loved. She slept on my chest the entire night. In the morning, I never thought in a million years that the little black kitten would be alive considering the condition she was in. Not only was she alive, she was rested and eager to eat. I rushed her to the vet, and they said her chances were slim and she would likely be blind if she did survive. I was determined to keep trying. After all, she had made it through the toughest first night.

In the morning, a volunteer walked in and was astonished she was still alive. I said, "I named her Hope."

Later that same day, a little duck came from an identical situation: his family was hit by a car. I put him in with Hope and they snuggled up against each other with full tummies, and went happily to sleep. Over the course of a few weeks, Hope would follow the baby duck around even though she was blind. They went on adventures together all around the house. Hope became stronger and stronger and eventually, she did have full vision in one eye. I named her seeing-eye duck "Jello."

The story was posted on social media and went viral as "Hope, the Little Blind Kitten, and Her Seeing-Eye Duck."

16

A Pig Too Far

A nd now a pig enters the story, because doesn't it always happen that way? A supersize boar named Bacon helped reinforce my decision to establish a charity and, later, to open to the public.

Raised for his meat, Bacon had been fattened to more than nine hundred pounds, way too big for his height and length. Just when he was "finished"—pushed to his top weight prior to slaughter—his tenderhearted owners realized they couldn't go through with it. And that's how Bacon ended up at the Funny Farm.

The poor boar was so heavy, he could barely move. Each day I had to plop down on the ground beside him, brace my feet against his back, and shove him to a standing position, in sort of a barnyard leg press. Only then could Bacon rise up and shuffle to the feed trough.

One morning, as I gave him the usual leg up, I felt a pull in my midsection, one of those "uh-oh" moments when you know you've hurt yourself. In a matter of minutes, the pain kicked in, and soon it felt like a knife in my side. When it didn't let up, I dragged myself to the doctor; if I'd learned anything from my mother, it was not to let routine health care lapse, though I had a hernia that I'd been faithfully ignoring for years.

"How did this happen," asked the doctor, "at the gym?"

"No," I said. "I was lifting a pig."

"Well, that's a new one for me."

He examined the painful bulge on my side, pressing it gently until I yelped. "Okay, Laurie, you now have two hernias, and they're not going to repair themselves. Don't take this lightly, because this sort of injury can lead to bigger problems down the road. It's time to look at a surgical solution."

As we did, I thought of my ongoing problem with uterine fibroids, which had only grown worse over time, causing unbearable cramps, intense bleeding, and a few very embarrassing incidents in the office.

Several times in the past I had inquired about an elective hysterectomy, but was refused because I was still in my thirties. The childbearing years. No matter how I insisted that I wasn't planning on having kids, I was met with a stone wall of resistance and was denied the procedure.

Now, at forty, I was fed up with the discomfort and inconvenience. I stormed into the office of my OB-GYN, and in no uncertain terms said, "While they're in there fixing those hernias, I want a hysterectomy. I have awful pain. When I bleed, it's like the prom scene from *Carrie*. I can't take it anymore."

Even then, she pushed back. "You know, Laurie, this means you'll never have children."

Little did she know. As far as I was concerned, I had hundreds of children, and they were just as messy and demanding and adorable and expensive as the human variety. Whatever motherly instincts I had were completely wrapped up in the animals at the farm.

"Doctor, believe me," I said, "I will sign a blood oath, swearing that I don't want children now and won't start to want them as soon as you do this procedure. Put me out of my misery, please. If you don't, I'm just going to go somewhere else."

Finally, I was permitted to choose the option that was best for me. I was scheduled for the dual surgeries, and they managed to squeeze me in before Christmas, so I'd be home for the holidays.

Back to back, the two procedures took more than five hours. Afterward, when I opened my eyes, Cathy and my boyfriend Dennis were there, bearing gifts and flowers, wearing relieved smiles. Dennis looked done in—he'd been there for the whole thing, slouched in the waiting room, taking quizzes in *Cosmopolitan*. Now, reassured that I was conscious and in the recovery room, he excused himself to go down to the cafeteria.

He had just waved goodbye when the heart monitor by my bed started to screech like a smoke alarm. With the sound, a weird tingling sensation swept me from head to foot, so strong that my feet and fingers felt like they were buzzing. Just before I lost consciousness, I dimly saw the door fly open and a group of attendants charge in, a small army in their green scrubs.

Then, fade to black.

At some point during the surgeries, someone on one of the medical teams had nicked a blood vessel and kicked off massive internal hemorrhaging. I wasn't out of the operating room more than an hour when I was rushed back in. Despite repeated MRIs and six more hours of exploratory surgery, doctors couldn't find the source of the bleeding, and therefore could not stop it. I went down like a toboggan, shockingly quickly. Inside a week, I was in the intensive care unit, and was briefly placed on a ventilator, one of the most unpleasant experiences of my life.

Cathy, bless her heart, kept a constant vigil at the hospital, and in an Academy Award–winning performance, told me, "Buck up, sis, you're going to be just fine." Dennis had a harder time masking his fear. The first time he visited me in the ICU, he took one look at me and he almost fainted. His eyes widened, and his skin turned the color of clay. My blood ran cold. Without saying a word, he told me I was dying.

It was confirmed when the attending physician told me that the source of my bleeding could not be identified, and nothing more could be done for me.

I can't die, I thought, just like Mom. *Who's going to take care of the animals?*

The next few days were a weird reckoning. Once again, I had to fast-track through those grief stages: denial, anger, bargaining, depression, and acceptance, and watch with mounting alarm as the hourglass emptied out.

I managed to take solace in the fact that, for all its challenges, I had loved my peculiar life and made the best of it. I wasn't necessarily afraid to die—I hoped I was going to see my mother—but sad to think how this would hurt my friends and family, and worried that I'd made no provision for the animals.

In a sense, I was conducting my own death watch when an older nurse lumbered into my room in the ICU. She must have been seventy-plus, short and stout—a little teapot—with curling gray hair and a businesslike attitude. She looked down at me as I huddled in my bed, trying to hold back tears.

"Come on now," she said, "what's wrong?"

"I'm going to die." I began to sob—big, raggedy, wet sobs.

With a brief shake of her head, she lifted my wrist, then checked her watch and frowned at a blipping digital screen near the bed. "Now who told you that? All of your other numbers are fine. Heart rate, blood pressure, respiratory—all improving." She dropped my wrist and made a clucking sound with her tongue. "You're recovering. Your body is just a little slow catching up."

I gazed up at her as if she had wings and a halo. "Really? You're not just saying that? You mean I don't have to go into the light?"

"I've been a nurse for fifty years," she said tersely. "You're too healthy for this to kill you, and whoever said otherwise is full of bunkum." She handed me a wad of tissues, and I blew noisily into them. "Sometimes these doctors forget to look at the big picture," she said. "Just because you have one number in the pits doesn't mean you're dying. Just give it some time."

She really must have been heaven-sent, because from that very hour, I began to get well. Who can explain it? I guess my internal bleed decided to clot, and my innards to heal. Let me tell you, there's no feeling in this world like coming back from the dead. On Christmas night, still in pain but with spirits soaring, I went home. It was one of the best Christmases ever.

I had been told I would spend five weeks in recovery, in bed, off my feet.

"Now you have no choice but to slow down," said Dennis. "Think of this as a mandatory vacation. Relax and enjoy it."

For the first few days at home, I tried to do just that, vegging out on TV and reading. Luckily my sister, a few work pals, and some close friends were kind enough to show up, take over the farm chores, and give me a hand with the housekeeping and personal care. To the strongest of them, I explained how to do the Bacon leg press. "But be careful!" I warned. "Don't strain a muscle or get a hernia."

In the end, I was constitutionally unable to loll in bed for five weeks. I was up and around in three, and got a golf cart so I could drive around the farm at a snail's pace and see all the members of my family.

The episode reinforced a few lessons I had already begun to learn. It was great to be self-sufficient, but I also had to be willing to accept help, happily, wherever it came from, whenever it showed up. I had to admit I couldn't raise hundreds of animals all on my own, with no assistance. I needed to stop keeping secrets.

And, wonder of wonders, in 2012 the Funny Farm Rescue and Sanctuary was approved to become a 501(c)(3) nonprofit charity.

From the start, I was blessed with an exemplary board of exactly two people. First, a longtime South Jersey wildlife rehabilitator named Vicki Schmidt joined as vice president. Then a lifelong friend and former work colleague named Diena Seeger volunteered to be secretary/treasurer. Diena's a serious businesswoman, a statistical mathematician with all the financial and business expertise. Curiously enough, she's afraid of most animals, or at least she was at the start.

"So what gives, Diena?" I asked her. "You don't live and breathe animals, like Vicki and me. Why do you want to join?"

"I want to be part of something great," she said, "working with someone who's passionate about what she does. That's you, Laurie. Count me in."

I am the president, or as I refer to myself, shit-shoveler-in-chief.

So when people ask how the Funny Farm became a "real rescue," I say it's a three-part answer involving a big feed bill, a big health scare, and—last but not least—a very big pig.

Diena learned of a three-day workshop offered at the Helen Woodward Animal Center in California and suggested we attend. It was called "The Business of Saving Lives." I checked out the center's website, and its motto appealed to me: "People help animals, and animals help people." I sure agreed with that. I signed up for the course, and off we went.

The program was tailor-made for people like me, who wanted to do more to help animals but were clueless about how to begin. The speakers there explained how business techniques—marketing, public relations, fundraising, social media—can apply to animal welfare organizations and help them to sustainably grow. We were lucky enough to get a sit-down with the center's president and chief executive, a globally renowned animal welfare expert named Mike Arms.

During our one-on-one meeting, I gave Mike the basics. The Funny Farm had just become a nonprofit charity. A few people, mostly friends, had started volunteering here and there. We'd also held several fundraisers, basically parties with friends where I served pizza and beer.

He listened quietly, then said, "And how's this working for you so far?"

"Well, okay. Not great-okay. Just okay. For the fundraisers, we buy rolls of tickets, guilt people into buying them, and make enough money to buy ten bags of feed. But I really need that feed, so I'm happy about it!"

"And the workload?"

"I still do most of it myself. It takes about six hours a day—three before work, three after—to do the feeding, but it gets done. On my days off, I get around to the rest: cutting goat hooves, cleaning stalls, restocking the hay, straw, and feed—"

Even describing it to him made me want to take a nap. "I do the best I can."

He nodded thoughtfully. "The problem is you haven't gotten serious about this yet."

My mouth dropped open. Not serious? Had he been listening? Wasn't I up at dawn every morning to do my chores before heading off to work? Wasn't I draining my savings each and every month in order to support my animals? Wasn't I running myself ragged to love and care for every last one of them?

I could have argued with Mike—I was tempted to—but I hadn't come to California to defend what wasn't working. He was the expert, not me. If I wanted to learn, I had to shut up and listen.

"Look, it's clear the animals have your heart," Mike continued. "But unless you run your rescue like a business—just like your other business, your graphic design company—you're going to go broke, sooner rather than later. Getting a tax break is the least of it. You've got to generate real revenue, as in donations—and I don't mean a kegger with friends. But you already know this, right?" He smiled. "Or we wouldn't be sitting here."

"I understand," I said. "I just don't think people I don't know will donate money to feed my animals. Why would they?"

"Trust me, when people find out what you're up to, they're going to support it. But you won't know that for sure until you stop hiding, open up the gates, and let in the world. Laurie, you've got to go public."

Immediately, I began to shake my head. "Oh, no. I don't want to take it that far. The Funny Farm is my home, not a petting zoo. I live there. And I'm telling you, when I get home at night, dog-tired and dragging my butt, the last thing I want to do is let in the world."

He nodded. "I get it. Your choice. But remember this. You can save a couple of hundred animals, or you can save millions."

"Millions?" Now he sounded nuts. "I don't even know what you're . . ."

"You've heard the saying, 'Save one life, save the world.' Kindness begets kindness. Small efforts inspire larger ones. If you stand up for mercy and compassion, others will stand with you. The ripple effect just goes on and on."

"But I have fifteen acres in the Jersey Pinelands. This isn't some big-deal operation. And quite frankly, Mike, I'm not out to save the world."

He leaned forward, looking at me intently. "Why not?"

I thought a lot about it on the flight home. I'd learned a lot at the workshop, which gave me some ideas about how to support the larger mission of animal welfare. But opening to the public? "Letting in the world," as Mike said, assuming that the world was interested in dropping by? I wasn't convinced.

But now the bug was in my ear, and as the weeks went by, I couldn't stop thinking about what he had said.

"Your choice. If you have something good, don't keep it hidden."

"You can save a hundred animals, or you can save millions."

And perhaps the most persuasive argument: "Sooner or later, you're going to go broke."

A thousand times I decided to take the leap. But I always got scared, and quickly undecided. Finally, I sat down with pen and paper, like my mom used to do, to list the pros and cons.

I knew the cons by heart:

I ran the real risk of surrendering my privacy.

I'd be overwhelmed by animals no one wanted. It would be torture to have to constantly turn them away.

The place would have to look nice every day! Wouldn't it?

What if no one was interested? It would be like giving a party and having no one show up. The thought made me feel weirdly shy and hesitant.

And then I started listing the pros. I thought this would be the short side of the ledger, but I had to admit, the benefits soon added up.

The animals might like seeing other people, because they sure didn't see enough of me. As a "working mom," I sometimes felt neglectful and guilty. It wasn't an ideal situation for any of us, and I often worried that I was shortchanging "my kids," the animals.

Also, wouldn't it be great if children came and met the animals, up close and personal? I felt this even more keenly in the digital age, when even little kids were becoming captives of technology, their worlds shrinking to the size of a smartphone screen.

Maybe I could get some help around the farm, as in volunteers, though it was hard to imagine that people would line up to muck out stalls and groom animals and build nesting boxes. Poop happens on a farm, and so does pee and spit and a whole lot of smelliness.

And maybe Mike was right, and I'd get a few more donations in the bargain!

Back and forth I went, agonizing over the decision—or the indecision. I wrote my list over and over, tore it up every time, then wrote it out again.

One morning, leaning in the farmhouse door with my second cup of coffee, I looked up at a pinpoint of light—a morning star, or maybe Venus—winking in the sky above the pines.

Mom, are you up there? What do you think I should do?

The following month, socked with another $4,000 feed bill (less 7 percent), I had my answer. With fear and trembling, and trembling and fear, I decided to go for it.

As much as I'd learned about marketing in California, I didn't do much to spread the word about our organization besides hang out my shingle and a sign at the front gate: Funny Farm Rescue and Sanctuary. For the longest time, not many people came by unless it was by accident. Seriously, at the start, that's how a lot of them discovered us:

"We were just driving around back here and saw your sign."

"We got lost in the Pinelands and wondered what's a Funny Farm."

"Is this place open? Can we come in?"

I started to wonder if anyone would ever visit on purpose but was happy to see that those who did, accidentally or otherwise, enjoyed themselves. Sometimes they dropped a few dollars in the donation bucket. Every cent of it was welcome. Every cent went directly to the care and feeding of the animals.

What the heck. If the most I got from my nonprofit status was a couple of bucks and a tax break, that would be fine with me.

Though the world did not rush in, I did manage to sweet-talk some friends into volunteering, including several friends from work. They would drop by for a few hours to feed and water the animals, collect the freshly laid eggs, brush the horses, goats, and steers, and scrub out the feeders. I was sure they'd bail after a single day, especially when they got a load, literally, of manure scooping. But most of them came back for more. When I asked why, I got variations on these answers:

"I like being outdoors."

"It's hard, but it's somehow relaxing. My stress just melts away."

"Why spend an hour on a treadmill when I get a better workout here?"

"The Funny Farm is my happy place."

And just as Mike Arms had predicted, more people started to show up. It wasn't quite a world of people, and it happened very slowly, but it happened.

Animal Tails

Angel and Steven

With so many dogs, alpacas, llamas, and donkeys on the grounds, the usual predators—foxes, owls, bobcats, coyotes, eagles— usually don't bother us.

One of our angel-wingers is a white Embden goose that had been permanently disabled in a car accident and couldn't walk at all. We called her Angel, but she didn't live up to her name. She had a chronically pissed-off disposition. I wasn't surprised at her unhappiness. Geese are extremely social animals who live and travel in flocks. For her own safety, Angel had to be in a coop, and watched mournfully from the sidelines as the other birds roamed freely around her.

Worse, though Angel hollered for attention all the time, when people approached her pen she acted aggressively, squawking and trying to bite through the chicken wire. One of our volunteers always doted on Angel, but couldn't possibly give her the love and social interaction she so clearly longed for.

For two full years Angel lived that way, so miserable that sometimes I wondered if I would be doing her a favor to put her down.

I was soon to discover that hope was a thing with feathers. Along came Steven, a healthy Canada goose who'd quit his own flock and started hanging around Angel's place (in case you're wondering, yes, geese of different species flock together, and have even been known to mate).

From the start, it excited Angel to have a companion. Though Steven couldn't enter the coop, whenever he stopped by, she would flap those mangled wings like crazy. And he would just roost there, content to gaze at her.

On a hunch, one day I opened up the door of the coop, then tiptoed away and hid, curious to see what would happen.

When Angel's volunteer friend walked by, she was concerned. "Who left Angel's pen open?" she demanded. "Steven is going to hurt her."

"Let's give it a try," I said. "Everybody likes to have a little company. Maybe he wants to help her. If they don't get along, we're no worse off than we were."

You can probably guess by now that Steven had no intention of harming Angel. With the coop door open, he edged a little closer to her, then closer still, until they were side by side. It seemed that he was standing guard at the entrance, like a sentinel. For the next couple of weeks, that was their routine. It was like a courtship.

Then came the day I spotted Angel sitting with Steven—outside the coop. How had she gotten there? I turned to mush when I saw her struggle to her feet and start walking—slowly and with great difficulty, but walking, right alongside her beau. I like to think that he encouraged her, saying, "C'mon, girlfriend, take a chance!"

Angel vacated her coop, and we repurposed it to house one of our skunks.

And so the angel-wing goose who didn't walk for years is back on her feet, thanks to the friendship of another goose. Angel's gait is kind of lopsided, like Charlie Chaplin, and she's pigeon-toed, but she keeps getting better and better. These days, you'll even see her running, all around the farm, rejoicing in her freedom—with Steven.

17

Chucky

By 2013, more than three hundred animals lived with me at the farm, every one of them a rescue. The grounds were overrun with squawking ducks and geese. The barn teemed with cats, feral and tame, along with all the farm animals. And I had two rescue dogs, a goofy Labradoodle named Freddie and a black Lab named Snoop.

As I had anticipated, it was an unusual day when I didn't get an earful of hard-luck stories. A skinny stray mutt roving in the woods. A litter of kittens dumped along the highway. A pen full of underfed but rapidly multiplying bunnies. Could I help?

Though lots of people knew I did rescue, my little sanctuary in the woods was still pretty much undiscovered; I had my tax break and a few donors, but no steady funding, public or private. I still paid for everything out of pocket: vet bills, equipment repairs, and upkeep of the farm.

One evening, after paying the bills, I declared to Dennis, "Enough is enough. I can't take in any more animals."

"I think I've heard that tune before."

"No, really." I fanned a stack of bills in his face. "For one thing, I can't afford it. For another thing, I *really* can't afford it."

Then came Chucky.

* * *

Barbara was a sixtyish single woman who worked in the video production department. One day around the office, I overheard her gabbing about her new German shepherd puppy, Roscoe. When she mentioned that he'd come from a breeder—she was so proud of his pedigree—I had to bite my tongue. With all the animals in shelters, why not adopt a dog?

But the deed was done. Besides, as Dennis often reminded me, it was none of my business. Until it became my business.

A few days later, Barbara buttonholed me in the hallway, her face filled with concern. "Hi, Laurie, you're the animal person, right? There's something weird going on with this puppy of mine. He throws up, constantly."

"Well, he's a baby, Barb. Babies throw up sometimes."

"No, this is different. This dog vomits every day, after every meal, I'm talking nonstop." She wrinkled her nose. "It's gross."

The obvious question: "Have you taken him to a vet?"

"You think I should?"

"I think you should."

A few days later, she popped into my office. "He has this condition called"—she squinted at a scrap of paper—"megaesophagus? The esophagus is too big or something? So he really can't get his food down." She looked at me expectantly, as if this were already *our* problem, not hers alone.

Laptop open, I did a quick Google search. As the term suggests, in animals with megaesophagus, or "mega-e," the esophagus is oversize, so the muscles can't propel food and water from the throat into the stomach. It's been likened to a balloon that's overinflated, and then hangs limp. There is no cure, though the condition can be managed with medication, special feeding techniques, and, sometimes, a feeding tube.

"Jeez, Barb, no wonder Roscoe's upchucking all the time. The poor thing can't swallow his food." According to the website, the condition is more common in dogs than in cats, more common in German shepherds than in some other breeds, and has been linked to inbreeding.

Aha. Inbreeding.

Don't get me started on breeders. I'm sure many of them—I hope most of them—are legitimate, ethical, and responsible. But I find it hard to support making new pets when there are so many homeless ones, either in shelters or on the streets. Besides that, any numbskull knows that animals bred from the same litter or bloodline could have health problems like little Roscoe's. In my opinion, if you breed littermates, you're no better than a puppy mill—if that.

"Boy, Barb," I said, "it looks like you've got a big job on your hands. Roscoe's going to need tons of extra care."

The drama played out pretty quickly after that. Barbara called the breeder and demanded two things: that she return her six hundred and fifty bucks and take back the sick puppy. The answers: yes and no. Barbara got her refund. But the kindly breeder said, "I don't care what you do with that puppy. I don't want it."

As Barbara gave me the update, I could just hear Dennis's voice in my head: "Tune it out, Laurie. Don't sign up to solve the problems of the world."

With my best I-feel-your-pain-but-don't-expect-me-to-take-this-animal look, I said, "Keep me posted, and if there's anything I can do to help . . ."

She shrugged. "Thanks. I'm going to take him to the pound."

"Say what?"

I had to stop myself from grabbing Barbara by the shoulders

and shaking some sense into her; instead I fixed her in my sights, forcing her to look straight into my eyes.

"Barbara, hear me on this. The pound will *never* adopt out a dog with this condition. Legally, they're probably not allowed to. Not only will they euthanize that dog—*your puppy*—but he will be very first on the list."

"Oh, no, really, Laurie. You haven't seen this little guy. He's so cute. And he's purebred!"

"You mean inbred."

"Maybe, but that's certainly not my doing. I wanted a guard dog, not some hardship case. And I really don't have time for all this hassle."

By sheer force of will, I stalked back to my office, quietly shut the door—I wanted to slam it—and tried to concentrate on my work. But I was simmering, and the angel and devil on my shoulders were already duking it out.

Think of that poor pup, murmured the angel, in a voice a lot like Mom's. *So helpless. Barbara will take him to the pound, and that's the end. They'll send him straight to death row.*

The devil argued back, in a voice a lot like Dennis's. *Not your problem! Not your job!*

The dogfight went on all day, back and forth, back and forth. By six o'clock, my stomach was doing the Macarena, and I couldn't wait to get the hell out of there. I locked up my office, waved goodnight to my coworkers, and promised myself a nice margarita when I got home, extra tequila. That would take the edge off.

I was inches from the exit sign when I came to a dead stop. Then I spun on my heel, as if someone had physically turned me around and propelled me in the other direction.

I stalked down the hallway toward the video department and pushed through the double glass doors. Barbara looked up from her editing bay, and I heard myself sigh, "All right already! Bring the dog in tomorrow."

Chalk one up for the angels. And for Mom.

The next day, Barbara strolled into my office, a gym bag slung over her shoulder. With a conspiratorial glance, she unzipped the bag, and there he was: a little ball of puppy fluff, all big eyes and swiveling ears and quivering pink tongue. When I lifted Roscoe into my palms—he was that teeny—I could plainly feel the bones under his fur. He was underfed and undernourished. He was also lively, curious, and full of puppyish energy.

And yes, he was really, really cute.

I could tell Barbara had already released him emotionally. "Thank you so much for helping out," she gushed, pressing my hand. "Here's twenty dollars for food, the least I can do. And oh, better get a pair of earplugs—industrial strength."

"What for?"

She rolled her eyes. "Honest to God, Laurie. This dog whines all night long."

It was after dark when I pulled into the dirt driveway in front of the farmhouse. The porch light was on, and the TV glowed blue through the window blinds.

Inside, I found Dennis dozing on the couch, the remote control balanced on his chest. Freddie and Snoop were piled up around him like furry throw rugs while a baseball game played across the screen.

Good. I might as well leave it till morning to introduce Roscoe.

I tried tiptoeing toward the bedroom, but a creaky floorboard gave me away. The dogs perked up. Dennis stretched. His drowsy smile faded when he saw the puppy in my arms.

I was already on the defensive. "Now, don't you start with me, Dennis. This puppy has a medical problem, and his owner can't take care of him."

"Oh, yeah? So why does it follow that you have to do it?"

He was on his feet in an instant, wide awake and pacing as Freddie and Snoop jumped up to sniff out the new arrival.

"For Christ's sake, we're up to our eyeballs, Laurie. You said so yourself. You're running yourself into the ground to keep this place going. We can't even take a vacation because—oh yeah, my girlfriend has three hundred frickin' animals at home! When is it going to end?"

Then he stopped in his tracks, eyes narrowing. "What kind of medical problem?"

At first, I hedged. "Sort of a digestive thing."

"What kind of a digestive thing?"

Oh, what the hell. It was pointless to sugarcoat it. "He can't swallow food. He regurgitates all the food he eats."

"You have got to be kidding me."

"Dennis, he was headed for the pound. They would have killed him."

"I don't care. I don't want any puking puppies in this house!"

I called it Baby Boot Camp.

Having Roscoe was like having a newborn, except this newborn had to be fed on the hour, almost around the clock, just to make sure he got enough nutrition to survive.

The best way to feed a dog with megaesophagus is to use a sort of doggie high chair called a Bailey chair. It was invented by Donna and Joe Koch, whose dog Bailey—also a German shepherd—had mega-e. Like a high chair, a Bailey chair has a shelf-like table in front that makes the dog sit upright, kind of like a person seated at a dinner table. That way, when you feed him, gravity takes over, and the food has no place to go but down.

It would have been impractical to get a Bailey chair for a puppy Roscoe's size, so I improvised. At every feeding, I buckled him into an infant car seat that I borrowed from my friend and pulled the straps as snug as possible across his chest. Because he couldn't take in solids, I used my blender (bye-bye, margaritas!) to mix up a sloppy gruel of Puppy Chow and water—sort of a doggie milk-shake. Then I poured it in a squeeze bottle and hand-fed him.

He happily slurped down the mix, but as Barbara had warned, most of it came right back up again, splashing all over the car seat, my hands, and the floor.

Every mealtime would be a multistep process, and a messy one: strap Roscoe in, mix the food, squirt it into his mouth, wipe away what came back up, and then do it again, multiple times in one sitting. He had to remain seated in his chair for up to an hour after each feeding, to better ensure that what went down didn't come right back up.

No wonder Barbara couldn't handle it—this dog was the champion upchucker. On the spot, I renamed him Chucky.

That first night, I fed and refed Chucky until I was confident he was full, then tucked him into a crate with a soft blanket and a couple of chew toys. "There you go, little guy. Sweet dreams."

I knew Barbara had left Chucky on the first floor of her house while she slept on the third. No wonder he'd cried. He probably had been lonely—and famished. I hoped having a nice full belly would make it easier for him to go to sleep.

I trudged into the bedroom, so flat-out tired I just kicked off my heels and collapsed on top of the covers, still in my work clothes, a black-and-white dress now splotched with liquid Puppy Chow.

Dennis had his back to me, pretending to sleep. I could almost hear him clenching and unclenching his jaw. He was seriously pissed, and I didn't blame him. He was overwhelmed. So was I. We didn't have time for each other, much less all the farm animals. And now a disabled puppy.

I rolled over in his direction. "Den . . ."

That's when it started: a tiny, high-pitched yip from the crate in the next room.

I fell back on the pillow and stared at the cracks in the ceiling, silently begging Chucky to drift off. But the pathetic cries—almost like the mewling of a kitten—didn't let up. Dennis was seething. I stood it for all of ten minutes before dragging myself back out of bed, staggering into the kitchen, and lifting Chucky from the crate.

"Don't you bring that puking puppy into this bedroom!"

"Damn it, Dennie, do you want him to cry all night long?"

I tossed a fleecy towel into a cardboard box, put the box on the floor on my side of the bed, and tucked Chucky inside. He nestled his head under my palm, and we both slept.

Until he was hungry again, one hour later.

This would be our routine, almost every hour at the beginning, though eventually we would whittle down his feedings to eight or nine times a day. Soon I was owl-eyed from lack of sleep, and lurched around at home and the office like the living dead. Once I dozed off in a business meeting, eyes wide open like a rag doll's, and had to be nudged awake by a colleague so I could deliver my presentation.

Chucky needed twenty-four-hour care, so I went on bended knee to friends, my sister, and Funny Farm volunteers, pleading with them to babysit while I was at work. It was the ultimate thankless duty—the hourly feedings, the spewing food, the clean-ups. To this day, I bless each and every person who pitched in to keep that puppy alive those first few months.

But they loved Chuck, who was almost heartbreakingly grateful for his food. Every time the car seat came out, his little tail would go into overdrive, his whole body would tremble with joy, and his mouth would open wide, like a baby bird's: food, at last! The poor little guy had been starving his whole life.

In the beginning, Chucky stuck to me like Velcro, but soon he became a devoted little brother to the big dogs, and trotted after them as they did their farm rounds. He discovered the Frisbee, and anyone who made that first throw was committed to at least a half hour of play. His energy was boundless. He looked rounder and more bright-eyed by the day.

But if he ate even a nugget of hard food—if he raided Freddie or Snoop's kibble, for example—it went badly for him. He would fall into an almost seizure-like fit of coughing as his beleaguered body tried to expel the food.

There had to be a better way. Barbara's veterinary report had been little more than a diagnosis. I needed a long-term solution. I called my vet in Mullica Hill.

"You can't fix mega-e, surgically or any other way, but a lot of dogs can live near-normal lives with extra care and the Bailey chair," the vet said. Then he lowered the boom: "I'm afraid Chucky isn't one of those dogs. He's got an unusually severe case, the worst I've seen. I know you don't want to hear this, Laurie, but sometimes, you have to make the merciful decision, for the animal's sake and for yours."

I was already shaking my head, and he shrugged. "I know, I

know. Get a second opinion. Get a hundred opinions. No one will tell you any differently."

I trusted my vet, but yes, I needed to have some consensus about this. So I drove Chucky to the Ryan Veterinary Hospital at the University of Pennsylvania, about two hours from home. Founded in 1884, it's a global leader in veterinary education, research, and treatment—these are the top docs in the world.

Their verdict was equally pessimistic. On a lighted screen, they showed me the X-rays, which revealed that Chucky's esophagus was nearly as wide as the pouch of his stomach. The situation was so extraordinary that several doctors and residents came through to look at the film, and made all sorts of huffing and hmm'ing noises, the kind that tell you a situation is really bad.

"Laurie, this condition is essentially terminal," said an internal medicine vet. "It would be kinder to euthanize the dog, so he won't suffer. He'll have zero quality of life."

That's when I knew he was wrong. "No quality of life? He's the happiest dog I know. Look, I'm doing the work, sitting him upright and feeding him constantly. He's gaining weight. He runs around and plays with the other dogs. He's the Frisbee king of the farm. He doesn't look sick, and he sure doesn't act that way."

"Getting enough food in him is just one of your problems. With mega-e, there's the risk of aspiration—food or water getting sucked into his lungs. Dogs like this have a higher risk of pneumonia. They can have internal anatomical damage, and even require feeding tubes. Let me spell it out for you, Laurie: he'll be sick a lot. You could incur a fortune in medical bills. And he won't live more than six months, tops. I realize you're attached to him. Think about this for a few days before you make a decision."

But I had already made it. "You say Chucky has six months? Then he has six months. And I'm going to make it the best six months ever."

* * *

I was paying a heavy cost in sleep deprivation. Day by day, I grew more stressed and short-tempered.

Dennis was still glum, and refused to help out with Chucky in any way, with one exception: he became the announcer, loudly broadcasting every time the dog had an accident, which he did regularly, from both ends.

In a voice like Ed McMahon's, Dennie would boom, "The dog upchucked!"

"Took a crap!"

"Peed!"

"Puke alert!"

"Another pile of poop in here!"

"Cleanup on aisle four!"

One day at mealtime, on my knees swabbing up the latest mess, I began to sob—great, racking sobs that bent me down almost to the floor. I hadn't cried like that since Mom died.

I'd hit a wall. I regretted bringing Chucky home. I hated myself for regretting it. Just how arrogant was I, anyway, to think I could always save the day? I hadn't saved Chucky at all. At three months old, his life was already half over. The condition was going to kill him, and all I'd done was make sure I had a front-row seat.

Meanwhile, I felt it was also killing me—not just the exhaustion, but the knowledge that I would soon lose Chucky, an animal I'd grown to deeply love.

I let myself cry, hard and long. From his car seat, Chucky whimpered with concern, trying to nudge me with his nose. I put my arms around him and cried some more, my tears muffled in the soft fur of his neck.

Eventually I realized Dennie was in the doorway, looking down at us, his expression an inscrutable mask. Finally he exhaled and said, "For Christ's sake, Laurie, you look like a zombie. Give me the bottle. Go take a nap."

I was too spent to argue or even be surprised by his offer. I stood up, washed my hands and face, and headed for the bedroom as Dennis squatted down in front of Chucky's seat.

"All right, you little mess-maker," he grumped. "Can you kindly point your projectile puke away from my face?"

The next day, in the kitchen where Chucky's car seat used to be, I almost tripped over a new Bailey chair, beautifully carved of fresh-smelling pine.

"Dennie! Where did you get this? Did you buy it?"

He snorted derisively. "Now, why would I pay for something I could build myself?"

A couple nights later, coming in from work, I had to stop short in the doorway. Dennis snoozed on the sofa as usual, Freddie and Snoop piled around him as usual, the ball game on TV as usual. And there, sprawled across Dennie's broad chest, was Chucky. His little paws were actually wrapped around Dennie's neck, and he had a look of sheer bliss on his puppy face.

I snickered at the scene for a few moments and managed to take a pic with my cell phone. Then I deliberately slammed the door, making everyone jump.

Dennis blinked. He looked startled, then annoyed. "Hey! Get this puking puppy off me."

Chucky leaped down from the sofa and bounded over to me, his tongue lolling, his tail happily switching the air. I scooped him up and laughed.

"Dennie," I said, "you are so busted."

* * *

Chuck quickly understood that he had to sit upright in his Bailey chair in order to eat. On busy mornings, it helped a lot that he learned to balance his bowl between his paws and have his breakfast without help from me. Then he'd be out the door, as frisky and energetic as his big brothers, Fred and Snoop.

We learned Chuck had a gift for settling farm disputes. Any time a fight broke out, our meddlesome geese would invariably start honking, and that was the cue for Chucky to go in and bust it up. We called him our Director of Security, and with the help of the Geese Police, he managed to maintain order on the farm.

Six months came and went. Chucky was still doing great. He was undeniably healthy, and almost the expected height and weight for his age. When I took him in for a checkup, the vets were amazed—and more than happy to admit they'd been wrong about his chances.

Maybe my mother was looking after him, because he continued to pull off her kind of miracles, defying expectations, outfoxing them all, and living far longer than we had dared to hope. Eight months. A year. Eighteen months. Two years. With every benchmark, he was living proof that it was possible to have a good life in spite of a disability, and it dawned on me that he could help teach that lesson to others.

The very next visiting day, we hauled the Bailey chair outside and staged a demonstration for our visitors. We shared Chuck's illness and limitations. We explained how we'd learned to manage them. I made my joke about no more margaritas in the blender, and the grown-ups had a good laugh. Then the star of our show backed into his seat, grabbed his bowl, and gobbled down his milkshake.

To my surprise, the Chucky Show became one of the most popular activities on the farm. We used his story to help kids understand that it's okay to be different or have special needs, and to ask for help when you need it, just like Chucky did.

We also emphasized how important it is to be kind, to help others who aren't as strong, and to stand up against cruelty and bullying. All those messages go together, and with Chuck's help, the kids took them to heart.

And so that once-helpless little pup, who was twice condemned to die, who stole my heart like no other dog before, became one of the Funny Farm's first and most celebrated ambassadors.

Animal Tails

Nikki

What's it like, having a cockatoo living in the house?

For one thing, it's earsplitting (the shriek of these exotic birds has been measured at 130 decibels, the same noise level made by a jet taking off from an aircraft carrier).

For another thing, it's a lifelong commitment, and then some (cockatoos can live to be eighty years old or even older!).

For a third, fourth, and fifth thing, having a cockatoo (or parrot, same thing) can be trying, exhausting, and messy.

Cockatoos have been likened to bratty children who never grow up. They demand lots of quality time with their favorite people. If they don't get it, they can become destructive and aggressive, and I can assure you, you don't want to tangle with an angry cockatoo. As I know from personal, painful experience, the bite power of this breed has been measured at more than 350 PSI (a Doberman pinscher, by contrast, comes in at 305).

And that, in a nutshell, is our Nikki. She's gorgeous, a Moluccan cockatoo with ivory plumage and satiny, coral-colored crest feathers that are almost flamingo pink on the underside. Like many birds of her kind, she was adopted and rejected, adopted and rejected several times before finding a home at the Funny Farm. Her former owners found her too demanding, too destructive, and too loud, with a high-pitched cry that can sound like a fire alarm.

Nikki was young when I took her in, only six years old, but she had already had three different homes. She doesn't have many language skills (or, more correctly, language-mimicking skills). She says "hello" in the most beguiling way, in a voice like Mae West's. She also has learned to say the names of some of our dogs. When anyone in the house laughs, she laughs along. If I get angry or frustrated, Nikki matches me in tone and attitude.

You're welcome to visit our Nikki at the Funny Farm, but please think carefully before bringing a cockatoo or any other exotic bird into your home. These birds can be lovely, fulfilling companions but they require—and deserve—tons of care and love.

18

Act Two

I hadn't seen my father since that day he'd ogled me in the check-out line, decades earlier. Our paths hadn't crossed, though we lived in the same neck of the woods. I'd heard nothing from him after Mom died. Truth to tell, he rarely crossed my mind. As far as I was concerned, he was spilled milk—my biological parent, but part of my past. It had never occurred to me that he might want to see me again.

Then in 2017, a distant cousin on the Zaleski side visited the Funny Farm. As we caught up with each other's lives, he said, "How would you feel about Rich coming by one of these days?"

At first, the name didn't even compute. "Rich who?"

He looked puzzled. "Umm, Rich Zaleski? Your dad?"

Just like that, my blood pressure spiked to fight-or-flight in seconds. After all those years, my dad still had the power to unsettle me.

Vince must have gauged my reaction, because he backed right off. "Hey, no pressure, Laurie. I get that he wasn't father of the year. It's just that he's heard about the farm, and I think he'd like to see it for himself."

I didn't know what to say, and surprised myself by blurting out, like a public service announcement, "The Funny Farm Rescue and Sanctuary is open to the public two days a week, Tuesday and

Sunday. Visiting hours are eight a.m. to four p.m. Admission is free."

As soon as I said it, I wanted to snatch back the words. But what the hell. I would not prevent my father from visiting the Funny Farm. I would not explicitly invite him. If he showed up, he showed up.

Sure enough, he showed up.

Visiting days are usually jam-packed, especially on Sundays, especially in nice weather, when it's not uncommon for hundreds of people to stop by the farm over the course of eight hours—a far cry from the early days, when I was thrilled to get a single carload.

The following Sunday dawned sunny and cool. All morning, a steady stream of cars rolled through the gates, driving one mile an hour, per the speed limit, to keep animals and children safe.

I spotted a champagne-colored Cadillac and braced myself. His blond hair was now ashy gray. His eyes were still a brilliant blue. Though something about him was different, I couldn't quite put my finger on it; it wasn't until years later that I found out that he'd had a nose job and an eyelid lift. All in all, he was fit and looked pretty much the same as I remembered.

He craned his head, scanning the crowds. When our eyes met, he raised a hand in recognition, then began to cry. It was in that moment—it couldn't have happened a moment sooner—that my apprehension dissolved. I no longer felt panicky or uncomfortable. I felt nothing.

Let him cry, I thought. *I finished my crying years ago.*

Pasting on a smile, I walked over and embraced him, smelling his cologne and the starch in his shirt. Our conversation was like one between strangers. Polite banter. Mindless chitchat. How was

I doing? How was my business? Just how many animals did I have here? How were my brother and sister?

Fine, fine, fine.

As I looked at him smilingly, I couldn't help but remember the torment he had inflicted on my mother, during and after their marriage. I remembered the times he cut our electric lines and water lines, depriving us of the little we had in this world. And when he reached out to touch one of the horses, I flashed back to Shannon O'Leary, dead on the ground, with two bullet wounds in his skull.

"I hear your mom passed," he said in a somber voice.

"Yes, she did," I replied.

He dipped his head slightly, checking that conversational box. He offered no condolences, but launched into details of his own active social life—his travels, his hobbies, his dance lessons. It seems he was in great demand as a ballroom and polka dancer. I wasn't surprised. Always the ladies' man.

Many years ago, I made up my mind that, even if a person is 95 percent bad, you focus on the 5 percent that's good and decent—that's what you hold on to. I was inclined, at least philosophically, to give my father the benefit of the doubt. Maybe he had done some soul-searching (I learned that in the mid-1990s, he was fired from Camden County College for sexual harassment). Maybe he was sorry for his past wrongs, had come here to say so, but couldn't quite spit out the words. Maybe it had been hard for him to reach out first. Dad wasn't the type of guy to swallow his pride.

But try as I might, I couldn't find it in my heart to care.

He stayed about an hour, and a volunteer took a photo of the two of us, smiling, saying cheese, like we used to in those family portraits. Before he left, we exchanged telephone numbers, and he made noises like he wanted to keep in touch. It was okay by me. Maybe there was an act two somewhere down the line, and this was the overture. Maybe the next time, we'd talk about something beyond the weather and his dance card.

I never heard from him again.

When Cathy heard about the visit, she hit the roof. "After everything that bastard did to us, why would you give him the time of day?"

But I found it oddly satisfying, like putting the finishing touch on an illustration or a period at the end of the sentence. In a curiously detached way, I was glad to know I didn't harbor bad feelings toward my dad. Maybe it was better that way, to harbor no feelings at all.

====== Animal Tails ======

Reggie

A few summers back an animal lover in Haddonfield, New Jersey, called to say he had purchased a sheep to keep it from being slaughtered. Did we have room for him at the Funny Farm?

The request took me by surprise. Haddonfield is one of the wealthier communities in South Jersey, not at all rural, filled with historic homes, boutiques, and upscale restaurants. As it turned out, the sheep was owned by a family that practiced animal sacrifice as part of their religion (the legality of such rituals continues to be debated).

Maybe the lamb knew it was in for a bad end, because it broke free from the family's yard and, for the better part of a month, was spotted running around the elegant neighborhoods of Haddonfield and nearby Cherry Hill, grazing to survive, and stubbornly eluding capture.

As often happens in cases like this, the sheep became a local news story. Lots of townspeople argued that he shouldn't become a sacrificial lamb. He'd already saved his own life. Law enforcement and Animal Control apparently disagreed. They finally cornered Reggie, brought him down with a tranquilizer dart, and returned him to his owners. That's when the abovementioned animal lover family stepped in, offering three hundred dollars if the family would surrender the sheep. Then he called the Funny Farm.

For a moment, I hesitated. I knew lambs and sheep are more susceptible to disease and infection than some other farm animals, and I didn't want to endanger my own herds. I was also aware that someone had to take Reggie, and fast, or he would literally be dead meat. After doing my quick list of pros and cons, I jumped in my pickup truck and headed with a friend up to Haddonfield.

After I picked up the sheep and got him safely tethered on the cargo bed, we drove through downtown Haddonfield with its boutiques and art galleries and coffee bars. When we stopped at a red light, a couple of hayseed farmers in a mud-splattered pickup, people on the sidewalk noticed Reggie in the back.

"Hey," came a voice from a sidewalk café, "isn't that the sheep that escaped?"

"It's Reggie the sheep!" someone else shouted. "Is he safe? Are you taking him home?"

I nodded and waved, and people all up and down the street began to cheer. As the light turned green and we turned south for Mizpah, we felt like superstars. The family who bought him also made a generous donation to the Funny Farm and still visit him to this day. Like many animals at the Funny Farm, Reggie arrived afraid and has since adjusted nicely. He is a farm favorite among volunteers and visitors.

19

No Fences

It took about three years before the Funny Farm became really well-known in our immediate neighborhood, Atlantic County and South Jersey. One thing led to another. One visit led to another. Accidental visitors became intentional visitors, then told their friends. Gradually, we were discovered by church groups, whole busloads of people who would show up on Tuesdays and Sundays, which I laughingly called my days off.

As visitation grew, so did the ranks of our cherished volunteers. Friends of friends got involved. They were followed by scout troops, church and civic groups, and classes of schoolchildren. The next wave included older students who had to fulfill community service requirements to graduate or gain admittance into the honor society. Then came adults who had to complete community service hours due to minor criminal offenses. Of course, animal lovers always wanted to get in on the action.

Today, we have a team of more than one hundred regular volunteers—as old as eighty and as young as three. Many places like mine don't allow children that young to volunteer, but I say bring them all, get kids started on the right path early. They're our future. Any child accompanied by an adult is more than welcome to volunteer at the Funny Farm.

Our volunteers run the gamut, from a bereaved widow who took comfort in the company of pigs to a Vietnam veteran with post-traumatic stress disorder who found peace and purpose working with the horses. One woman who volunteered had been house-bound and depressed to the point of suicide when a news story about the farm got her out of the house—for the first time in two years. She started to visit, and eventually became one of our most faithful and outgoing volunteers. "After years of confusion and self doubt, I have found a purpose," she told me later. "I bond with the animals when I can't find the voice to speak to people."

It seemed as if the right people showed up at the right time, as if I had special-ordered them. Some were great at building shelters, like the Eagle Scout who made it his project to construct a large chicken coop, and a local Girl Scout troop who built us a skunk house and plenty of animal pens. Sometimes, companies would bring dozens or hundreds of employees out as part of team-building initiatives. Astonishingly, freed from their cubicles and conference rooms, they seemed to get a big kick out of doing farm chores, including the ultimate character-builder, scooping the poop.

Once, a giant trailer hauling three hundred hay bales pulled into the gate just as a big nor'easter was moving in. I was frantic; if we didn't unload it fast, the hay would be soaked, and we'd have no choice but to discard it, at a loss of more than a thousand dollars. Desperate, I jumped on Facebook and implored anyone who was close by to please come help. Within twenty minutes, a team of construction workers showed up, looking like the lumberjacks in *Seven Brides for Seven Brothers*, ready for a barn-raising.

"It's our lunch hour," the foreman said. "Tell us what to do."

All I had to do was point to the trailer piled high with orchard grass hay. Without another word, they got to work, and like fire-men on a bucket brigade managed to unload and store the hay just as the first raindrops started pelting down. Other companies have come in to help with big projects like fixing fences and repainting the barn.

We took a great leap forward in 2016 when we (finally) got serious about our social media presence, with the help of volunteers who had a flair for Facebook and Instagram. I was astonished the day we exceeded 10,000 Facebook friends. Of course, it all grew exponentially from there, through word of mouth and online.

Mike Arms had been so right: when people found us, they loved us. They loved our animals and wanted to support them. Collectively, pitching in with their time, talents, and enthusiasm, they are the engine that keeps us running and helps us grow.

Soon enough, local school districts asked if we offered a traveling educational program, something we could take to classrooms to share our message of kindness to animals, and to each other. I was reluctant at first—I was still a business owner and employer as well as a farmer, and didn't have time for one more thing—but a teacher friend kept after me until I said, "Okay, tell me when and where, and I'll show up with a few of the animals."

That first assembly sold me. Walking into a vast gymnasium with a few dogs, Adele the diva house chicken, and Billy the baby goat, I was welcomed by the soundtrack from *Vision Quest* booming from the sound system. This wasn't just a classroom. The whole school was there, eight hundred excited kids. I felt like we were rock stars going onstage to a bunch of screaming fans. I read an anti-bullying children's book about our rescue farm animals. Like the day Harry Hamburger came to my own school, it was a day these kids would never forget, some saying it was the best day of their lives. We taught messages of acceptance, teamwork, and getting along with others. That day, all the invisible fences that separate children—social caste, cliques, color, culture—just fell away. It was like magic. The children learned about animals and some of their stories describing how they had found a happy ending at the farm. The kids' responses were monumental. They laughed. They applauded. They cheered. And they appreciated the message.

"These are animals no one wanted, who were abandoned and sometimes not treated very nicely," I told them. "Now they're safe. They have hundreds of brothers and sisters who love them."

One little girl in pigtails asked, "Miss Laurie, how do the different animals all get along so well with each other?"

I said, "Sometimes they spat like brothers and sisters, like you probably do at home, am I right?" Heads nodded all around. "But they make up by suppertime, and they all get along famously. Farley here is buddies with a goat named Cowboy, a sheep named Reggie, and a cow named Yogi. We call them the Fabulous Four because they're always together. If these animals of all different species can get along despite their differences, so can we, don't you think?"

Word quickly spread, and we received numerous requests from other schools. Kids brought supplies and gathered donations for the animals. As the program ended, kids lined up to pet all of the animals. Their lit faces and sparkling eyes reminded me of how I felt when I was a girl. Most had never been so up close and personal to a farm animal before, and they gasped in excitement when Adele the diva chicken would stand on her brother Farley's back. My heart was warmed knowing that my animals, who once had little or no hope, were now living the lives of celebrities. Mom would have been so proud.

Having grown up dirt-poor in a middle-to-upper-class neighborhood, having been labeled "underprivileged" and felt the sting of that, this mattered to me—the message of acceptance, of not looking down on or bullying people who are different or because they have less.

How do you measure someone's worth anyway? My family may have had little money and fewer possessions, but we were rich in love and adventure and fun. When you're measuring advantages, those things count for more than net worth or square footage.

"Society says dogs don't get along with cats, a chicken can't be friends with a dog and a squirrel can't sleep with a bunny," I told the kids. "But they do at the Funny Farm. Because we let them."

Eventually, it wasn't uncommon for hundreds of people to show up on visiting days, and then thousands. Five thousand people came to our fall festival in 2017, and in 2018, twice that many came, until traffic backed up through the Pinelands and out onto Route 40. By way of apology, I made the rounds of my Mizpah neighbors, handing out muffins and fresh eggs and promising I'd manage the crowds better next time.

In 2019, the Funny Farm in the remote Jersey Pinelands—once my closely guarded secret—welcomed more than 100,000 visitors from as far away as the United Kingdom, Mexico, and even Russia. We now have friends across the state, around the country, and, to my everlasting, gob-smacked astonishment, around the world.

Some in the close-knit rescue community have urged me to keep barriers between our animals and visitors—think of the potential liability—but I've never believed in rescuing animals only to cage them. I've visited livestock farms and petting zoos where there were not one but *two* fences to keep people and animals at a distance, and kids can only feed the animals through a plastic chute. I mean, seriously, what kind of fun is that? At the Funny Farm, we believe that friendship has no fences.

Sometimes I've had to make adjustments, as with Yogi, who's

now pastured on visiting days because of his horns. But as much as possible, this is a free-range farm, and I plan to keep it that way. I'm not unmindful of natural rivalries in the animal kingdom, and I don't disregard the fact that a dog, given the chance, could show aggression toward a pig, or that a flock of roosters, given the chance, could love a hen to death. But whenever it's possible and safe, our animals are unleashed, untethered, and unrestrained. They all seem to know that they have all been given a second chance, and, once they get to know one another, strong friendships form. Sometimes, even the most odd friendships.

When I ask people what they like about the Funny Farm, most often they say, "I can't believe the animals just walk around together!" One visitor compared the Funny Farm to a Disney movie, "where all the woodland animals get along, and the birds hang up your laundry."

We added attractions, like hay wagon tours that rumble around the farm's perimeter pulled by a tractor; we go through the woods, around the cow and horse pastures, past the Kitty Kottage and Cat House and the Pig Village and the time-out pasture, where our retired racehorses live. I talk all about the farm and its origins, again without going into any of the animals' sad stories except to say they once had little or no hope, but now they live their best lives ever. We suggest a three-dollar donation for the ride, but it's never mandatory. In the past I've seen parents and kids back away because they thought there was a fee, but I emphasize that at the Funny Farm, everyone is welcome. One Sunday, I was heartsick to hear a dad ask a volunteer if his child could go on the ride alone, as he and his wife didn't have the few bucks they thought they needed to join her.

That wasn't going to work for me. Before the driver could rev up the tractor, I flagged him to stop, then jumped off the wagon and took the man aside.

"Sir, won't you please join us on the hayride?"

"Well, we don't have the money to spare right now . . ."

I wanted to tell him I'd been there, a lot: broke, dead broke, as broke as broke gets. But in his eyes, I saw the same awkward bashfulness I'd often felt in school, when the other kids had lunch money and I had to use a ticket. Or the time I couldn't afford to buy a book at the book fair, and had to settle for a bookmark. Or the day I had to admit to my teacher that we had no phone, and I could see in her eyes that she felt sorry for me. Back then, a couple of dollars in my pocket would have felt like riches, and pity, while borne out of kindness, was no help at all.

I didn't want to embarrass the man and his wife, so I just said, "Aw, come on, make my day and join us. It's a little ride through the woods, no big deal, and it's free. Don't you think your little girl would have more fun if you came along?"

It may be most gratifying for me and the volunteers to host schools from the inner city. A lot of these kids live in poor neighborhoods, marked by broken concrete, broken glass, and, sometimes, drugs and crime. For them, those things may be background—the norm, what they're used to, like rural poverty was for me. But to bring city kids to the country is to see miracles in real time. They're dazzled by everything—to see horses and pigs up close, to be out in the green of nature, to take a twenty-minute hayride through those rutted back roads.

I have to add that, while we never charge for field trips, many school groups do bring a donation of money or animal food. I was bowled over when one of the out-and-out poorest school districts in South Jersey mounted a collection campaign in which the kids went to all their relatives and neighbors and collected coins in jars for the animals at the Funny Farm. That school district, in addition to bringing along boxes of cat litter, rolls of Bounty towels, and tins of kitten food, also brought a bank filled with money—nine hundred dollars, more than we had ever received, even from the wealthiest district.

As I hugged the kids and looked into each young, hopeful face, I had to tip my head back, my old trick to keep the tears from spilling over. The trick isn't always foolproof. I saw firsthand the love they had for the animals. One of the most impactful and powerful things I have ever experienced or witnessed is the undeniable bond humans can have with animals.

On a winter morning in 2019, Chucky played a game of Frisbee, settled onto his fleece-lined bed on the front porch of the farmhouse, looked all around the farm, let out a long sigh, and died. Saying goodbye to so many animals over the years did not make saying goodbye to my Chucky any easier. Because of his megaesophagus, and all that we experienced together for more than five years, I was closer to him than any animal I have ever known. Thank God, I was still home, just inside the door, preparing to leave on a business trip to Washington. In tears, I called Dennie, who made a U-turn and rushed home from work. I had said in every Chucky demonstration to live each day to the fullest because tomorrow is promised to no one, and it hit me, we had done just that. I was grateful to Chucky for the time we had together. My life without him would never be the same. I knew Mom was there waiting for him.

The other dogs came over to see why I was crying. We had lost Snoop by that time, but all the other dogs—Freddie and two new dogs named Farley and Rocky—watched us dig a grave in the front yard, next to the place where Mom's ashes were buried. It was important to let the dogs see Chucky's burial or they wouldn't know where he had gone.

Gently, we laid Chucky's still-warm body into the ground, then filled in the grave.

To my astonishment, within minutes, the dogs dragged Chucky's bed and toys from the porch to the grave site and started to play on the mound of freshly dug earth. Chucky was gone, but they still included him in their game. At that, the floodgates opened. Dennie's face crumpled. He turned and strode quickly away.

In my mind, I heard Mom's voice: "Have a good cry, Laurie. The more you cry, the less you pee."

For six months, Chuck's Bailey chair gathered dust in a corner of the kitchen. For a while, I just didn't have the heart to move it out. But a Bailey chair serves only one purpose, and I knew I had to find another dog and owner who could make use of it. One weekend I pulled out the chair, dusted it off, and was preparing to post a photo online when I heard from a couple named Cindy and Mike, whose adopted German shepherd, apparently bred with her brother, had given birth to a litter of pups. Cindy and Mike were successful in finding homes for four of the pups, and kept the rest, including Tucker, who had a disorder called megaesophagus.

"Our vet said we should have him put to sleep," Cindy said. "Then a friend of ours who comes to your farm told us that you lost a dog with the same condition. Is there any chance in the world that you'd be willing to take Tucker?"

It seemed the natural order of things, like the seasons. Chucky had died in the winter. Springtime was for grieving. By the summer, Tucker was living at the Funny Farm.

Later that year, we decided to plant a tree to mark Chucky's grave— dogwood, of course.

The woman in the garden shop warned me that dogwoods in bloom can give off a kind of pungent, even unpleasant odor.

"Perfect," I said. "So did Chucky, most of the time."

We planted the sapling and staked it with a white picket fence to prevent the goats from eating it. It grew into a beautiful tree. It reminds me every time I walk out of my door of my wonderful dog, Chucky—who lived for more than five years.

===== **Animal Tails** =====

Socks

Socks was not just a big beautiful all-white horse who seemingly floated around the farm. He was known as the "Guardian Angel."

Socks was almost like an emotional washing machine. He took away your dirt, wrinkles, and stains. In a way, he made you see and feel things that you once only heard about when the world had no problems, like the "good old days!" He made you realize the "good old days" are right now, each moment, each breath of air we take. Somehow, he made it seem as if there is so much more to life than our minds can understand. He was a peacemaker made out of a giant bundle of pure love.

Socks roamed free at the Funny Farm for more than fifteen years and was one of the first animals to come to the Funny Farm's new location. He never liked being in a stall or fenced-in area yet he would never leave. He was no ordinary horse, not by a long shot.

Many visitors tell us the Funny Farm is one of the only places where they can go in this entire world and somehow forget about their troubles, their pains, and their sorrows.

It's the same for animals. The fear and sorrows the animals once faced are now distant memories partly because of the love they received from Socks. He was a true peacemaker and a giant source of warmth and love to everyone, humans and animals alike.

The love and compassion and excitement that the Funny Farm animals have each and every day is something you cannot deny when you stand among them.

If you could take a picture into another more perfect world, Socks was it. Here, you feel love like you've never known. You may have never realized what true, unconditional love was until you came to the Funny Farm and saw and touched Socks. If you ever felt sad or upset, you'd surely feel a nudge or a giant white head resting on your shoulder. People came from all over the world to see him and were starstruck by his presence.

One young couple walking around the farm was surprised to see Socks following them, and, every time they stopped, he'd gently nudge the wife's stomach. He did it repeatedly. No one knew why. A couple of weeks later, they returned and told us she was pregnant. Socks knew it. Imagine how that young couple felt.

When you first drove into the Funny Farm, it was a constant sight to see Socks standing at the gate waiting for you, like you belonged here the whole time.

He lived to be thirty-nine, an extraordinarily long life in horse years, and was so popular that when he died in 2018, it made the local news.

20

Valentine's Day

In late February 2020, I got the call informing me that my father had toppled down the staircase of his home and died. He was seventy-seven years old.

It had been more than two years since he'd come to the Funny Farm and cried real tears and promised to keep in touch. I had been open to a relationship with him, but wasn't surprised when he hadn't pursued it. I let it go.

In the moment, I was shocked. Saddened. But I would not describe what I felt as grief. It was more of an emptiness. I couldn't honestly mourn for the father I had lost. I guess I mourned for the father he might have been.

Cathy was unmoved. "It was Mom who pushed him down the stairs," she said.

Stephen called it karma, but he couldn't help crying a little bit, too.

The neighbor who phoned me was a Funny Farm visitor who somehow had put together that Dad and I were kin, though he'd insisted for years that he had no children. He hadn't been seen around the cul-de-sac for a while, she told me, but the neighbors thought nothing of it, as he had been planning his yearly jaunt to Cancún.

Then his mail started to pile up, so she asked a police officer who lived in the cul-de-sac to look in on him.

By the time he was found, Dad had been dead for several weeks. But they fixed the date of death as the day he was discovered: Friday, February 14. He died alone.

Richard Zaleski, my mother's valentine, was gone.

It was left to us, the phantom children, to clean out and sell his house. Driving into Timber Heights, the trees seemed much taller and the surrounding suburbs more sprawling. But the neighborhood itself was largely unchanged. And that went double for our childhood home at Timber Heights Court.

Opening the door to Dad's was like stepping into a time machine, set to the early 1970s. Everything was just as I remembered, down to the red shag rug, the popcorn ceilings, and the orange bathroom with the flocked wallpaper. The faux Tiffany lamps were still there, along with the Naugahyde-and-chrome swivel chairs. The kitchen was just the same: a built-in Magic Chef wall oven and Melamine counters that looked like slabs of Spam. He still had the pool table downstairs with multicolored balls racked up and ready to go. The same neon beer signs hung on the paneled wooden walls.

Even the kids' bedrooms were intact, still kids' bedrooms with the original furniture and bedding, as if we had just stepped outside to play.

I couldn't make sense of it. My father's actions, his years of violence and acts of retribution, all spoke of a hatred so intense that it demanded a blood price. But inside his house, it was as if time stopped when my mother left him.

* * *

Each visit to Dad's was like a weird treasure hunt. We uncovered troves of mementos of our lives together, including photographs of the family and spools of home movies. We found pictures taken before and after his plastic surgery, full face and profile. Unnervingly, there were stacks of photos of the original Funny Farm, including one of Mom (in a bikini and cowboy boots!) walking one of our school friends on a pony, plus shots of the big trash heap next door and all those rusted cars. Those were tucked away with paperwork showing that the photos had been taken by a private investigator. Dad had covertly watched us all our lives.

I also found letters written to him by my mother in the early days of their romance—sentimental, loving, sweet, and filled with hopeful plans. Some were so intimate I almost blushed to read them.

And in his bedroom, we found a .38 caliber Smith & Wesson revolver and a box of wadcutter bullets, the same kind of gun and ammunition used to kill Shannon O'Leary. Of course, we'd known for years that Dad had killed our horse, cold-bloodedly, mercilessly, and then left the body for his ex-wife and children to find.

Part of me wanted to say to hell with him, but I couldn't do it, not even then, when it would have felt so satisfying. Somehow it would have been too easy to hate a man who was so hollow inside. Dad had been pitiless. And for that, I pitied him.

As we discovered, he'd planned his funeral like he shopped for a new car. At the Turnersville funeral home, he'd priced a burial package complete with a titanium-steel casket—the Cadillac of caskets—plus a marble headstone, to be covered by a $10,000 burial policy. Then he took the quote, went to a rival funeral home in Blackwood, and challenged them to beat the price.

Hey, I'm frugal, too. Having done without for most of my life, there's nothing I love like a good bargain. It just seemed silly that my father—still a man of means at the time of his death—haggled about this final transaction, which was covered by insurance anyway. The man never changed his stripes. And guess what? He got a cut rate from the second mortician—$8,000 for the send-off of his dreams.

The funeral director also said Dad claimed to have no heirs. In a mournful voice befitting his profession, he showed us the insurance documents, with Dad's handwriting scrawled across the back: "No children," with the words underlined twice. Yet he left no will to disinherit us, so the house and its contents were ours. It took a month of Sundays to clear out and renovate the place before we put it up for sale, along with his champagne-colored Cadillac.

I took the responsibility of answering the messages on his answering machine, messages from the girlfriends' club. Dad's chorus line had grown older, but to the very end he had several ladies, all in perpetual waiting, each one unaware that the others existed. Those were interesting conversations.

"Hi, this is Laurie Zaleski, Richard Zaleski's daughter."

That announcement was usually met with shocked silence, followed by a sputtered, "But Richie has no children!"

"Yes, he does. Three, to be exact. And I'm sorry to tell you that our father has died."

Then I would have to comfort them, all of these lovely devoted women who were crying because he was gone. Well, at least there were people to mourn him. His dance partners.

Curiously, just one message of sympathy was posted on my father's online obituary. It described him as a wonderful guy and a great teacher who made learning fun for one and all. It expressed the hope that he had been reunited with his beloved wife, who had passed away many years earlier.

It made me wonder what kind of stories he'd spun about my mom all those years. Did he depict himself as a suffering widower? Did he really mourn her? It even made me wonder if he had another family stashed away somewhere.

By then, nothing about my father would have truly surprised me, but it would remain a mystery.

For weeks, Cathy, Stephen, and I pulled up old carpet and laid down new floors. We polished that house, we painted and pressure-washed it, top to bottom, then happily staked a FOR SALE sign on the lawn. On a whim one day—since I was in the neighborhood and this was a remembering time—I drove around the corner to see what, if anything, remained of the old Funny Farm.

Driving up, it felt surreal. The house itself had been demolished a year after Mom died. I half expected the rest of the woods to be gone, too, leveled for commercial development. To be sure, there were a whole lot more convenience stores and strip malls, gas stations and parking lots along the freeway. The Hitcharama (now Hitch RV) was still going strong. The other buildings and offices were there, too, occupied by a limousine service, a roofing company, and a beauty salon offering permanent cosmetics. (I think Mom would have liked that time-saving idea.)

But lo and behold, when I parked near the road and walked down what was once a long driveway, I saw that a lot of the old woods were still there, untended and growing wild.

It was a beautiful blue-sky day, with a light warm breeze. As I tramped back into those overgrown fields, I remembered how I used to bolt from the school bus and chase into those woods, coattails flying, so no one would have time to see where I lived. A Piney among the pines.

For the most part, the property had been wonderfully let alone,

I guess some would say neglected. I had to duck low-hanging branches and squeeze by thorn bushes to reach the clearing where we once had lived.

All the old cars were gone, though remnants of Mount Trashmore remained. As I walked deeper in, into knee-high and thigh-high weeds, the highway sounds seemed to fade in the whoosh of the wind. The fences had been taken down or had fallen down, so it was hard to tell where it all had been until I spotted part of a crumbled concrete foundation and some boulders poking out of the soft, muddy earth. The house was right here, and our firepit over there, and somewhere nearby, the bones of our beloved horse Shannon O'Leary and our other animals we loved so much.

When I was five years old and my mother first brought us here, me and my sister and brother, I thought of it as a way station, a place to be on the way to someplace else. Little did I know, I would end up spending most of my life here. This is where I watched my mom forge a new life and a whole new self, turning from a demure, manicured housewife to a latter-day homesteader, chopping wood and building fences while laboring at multiple low-wage jobs and coping with endless terrorism from her former husband. This is where I learned resilience, toughness, and the kind of compassionate generosity that leaves the door open for everyone. In short, this is where I learned to become a strong woman. Just like Mom.

Wandering around, I saw there were still tons of milkweed plants on the property, with the ability to draw swarms of monarch butterflies and with spiny pale green pods that in the fall would crack apart and throw off that wonderful fluff, like little angels or parachutes, and float in the air like snow.

As I stood there in the tall weeds, I reflected on my entire life. I could almost see Mom, Stephen, Cathy, and Gordon and all that we did. I remembered every story and adventure and hardship. To think of what I learned there and each lesson Mom taught me, I realize all that I have and all that I am came from this little shack in the woods. Mom made it a home. She taught us love, kindness to others, forgiveness, and standing up for what you believe in. She gave me drive and self-determination. I worked hard and learned lessons from Mom, some hard and some extra hard, none easy.

I always knew I would be an artist, but who knew I'd be a farmer, too? I always say, "Life happens when you're busy making plans." Sometimes, I wonder why things are as they are and how it all came to be. I used to joke and say I was going to live in Philly and have cappuccinos with my friends, but I ended up at the Funny Farm. Mom always said everything happens for a reason. I believe that the Funny Farm is where I am supposed to be. I have learned to embrace the challenges just as Mom did so many times. This was not what I had in mind for my life. Apparently, someone felt differently.

I do believe that Mom had a hand in the success of the Funny Farm and the miracles that happen here every day. One thing is for sure, she keeps me laughing. Like a flight instructor who says "fly the plane" while you're landing, you almost hear her voice every time you land. I remember one important lesson Mom taught me when I was a kid. When I had something important to do and my room needed cleaning up, which was always, she'd say, "Laurie, the dirt will still be there when you get back. Go have fun!" When I got home, I always cleaned it, and she always had high expectations, but she knew how to put life in the proper perspective. I have since always seen the humor in things, which has carried me through many tough situations in life.

I wish Mom could see the Funny Farm today—I'd like to think she can. She would be so proud. The Funny Farm Rescue & Sanctuary is the world Mom imagined, and this is only the beginning. You never know what you are capable of until the day comes when you have to go places you hadn't planned on going. I know I am not alone. Mom still inspires me in all that I do. Sometimes life happens just as it is meant to happen and isn't at all what we first imagined. Leaving the remains of that little shack in the woods was harder than I thought because of all that took place there. The memories will never be forgotten. It was my home.

My brother Gordon has since moved back from California and lives just down the street from the new Funny Farm Rescue and Sanctuary with his wife and four children. They have helped build the Funny Farm into what it is today, especially as things got busier and busier. My nieces and nephews are some of the hardest-working kids. I wonder where they learned that?

Now, I stand on the second floor of my gambrel-style red-and-white barn overlooking the entire Funny Farm and take it all in with a deep breath. Everywhere I look is a world of happiness. The Funny Farm Rescue and Sanctuary has never had a brighter or more exciting future. There are many stories left to be told, but the biggest story of all is how my mother, Anne Elizabeth McNulty, inspired me to be the woman I've become.

I will be forever grateful for everything Mom did for me and every sacrifice she made. Because of her, my life has been nothing short of incredible. She gave me the tools I needed to never give up and face any challenge with courage and inner strength.

I am looking forward to my next chapter, because my unexpected life with 600 animals can only be the beginning.

Someday

It's not quite daybreak on the farm, but I've been up for hours. As the first shards of light break through the pine boughs, I'm already dressed, well caffeinated, and ready to go.

In the living room, Nikki greets me with a crooning hello followed by a hellacious squawk. That's the cue for Tucker and Farley and all the other dogs to race for the door, where they clamor to go out. Adele stirs in her indoor henhouse so I lift her out, fit her with one of her stylish diapers, and spill some mealworms into a purple plate on the floor. A dozen cats and kittens dream on. Nemo the baby goat cries for his bottle.

I want to get a jump on the chores, which are truly never-ending on a farm. Bending my head against the morning chill, I walk past my secondhand truck, which came with the bumper sticker: PROUD TO BE A PINEY, FROM MY NOSE DOWN TO MY HINEY. I step carefully around flocks of still-slumbering ducks and geese. In the barn, I'm greeted by the soft nickering of horses, the hiss and purr of the feral cat colony, and playful headbutts from Cowboy, who wants to be fed immediately, if not sooner.

Now the birds are starting their early-morning racket. Somewhere out there, Ricky the peacock screams out a good-morning. The farm is officially awake, and everyone's hungry.

Better get a move on.

I toss a couple of flakes of hay onto the barn floor, scoop some grain into the feed buckets, and throw handfuls of cracked corn and chopped lettuce to the birds. It's going to warm up soon, and after that, it won't be long before the visitors start pouring in. The front gate swings open and, hurray, the first of the volunteers arrive. I'll leave it to them to let the horses into their pastures, feed the pigs, open up the souvenir shop, and try to get to the thousand and one other tasks, big and small, that have to be done every day at the Funny Farm.

That's when the phone rings, down deep in the pocket of my Carhartts. It's an anxious-sounding couple who have managed to round up a goat kid that was running wild in the suburbs of Camden County. The baby somehow escaped a truck bound for the slaughterhouse. Now she's made their backyard her hideaway and is busily exfoliating their bushes and trees.

"We managed to get her in the garage—at least we think it's a girl," says the woman. "She's awfully sweet, but we can't possibly keep her." She pauses, then asks tentatively, "Is there any chance she can live at the Funny Farm?"

Oh boy. I have eighteen goats now. That's a pretty full house.

She texts me a photo of the little black kid with white blaze and budding horns, looking timid and cornered in the couple's garage. She has wattles like teardrops on either side of her head; they look like pearl earrings.

I survey the volunteers, now busy at their chores. I wave to the first carloads of visitors, lining up at the front gate. It's sunny now, but the night lights continue to glimmer on the old buckboard wagon out front, the place where Annie McNulty is buried.

Well, Mom, here we go again, I think. *What do you think I should do?*

As if I had to ask.

"I'm pretty busy today, do you have a way to get her down here?" I ask. "I think we can find room for one more."

Acknowledgments

Thank you to everyone in my family, especially my sister Cathy, my brother Stephen, and my brother Gordon and his wife Jennifer and their children Mackenzie, Aidan, Hunter, and Madison for lifelong adventure, hard work, and friendship. Thank you to my aunts, uncles, and cousins who have loved me and supported my efforts throughout my entire life.

All of my incredible friends, encouragers, supporters, and donors who have sustained the Funny Farm Rescue and Sanctuary, in Mays Landing, New Jersey, through the good times and the bad times.

Without my ever-changing team of dedicated and devoted volunteers throughout the years, the Funny Farm would not have been possible. Thank you for sharing your time and talents, which directly contributed to saving the lives of hundreds and hundreds of rescue animals. You helped give them the lives that every animal deserves. All 600 animals are rescues, once with little or no hope. You helped make their stories inspirational. Although there are too many volunteers to mention individually, they all have my gratitude and love.

Thank you to all of our supporters from around the world. Due to COVID-19, most businesses including the Funny Farm were temporarily closed to visitors. We launched the Funny Farm Show, which broadcasts live on Facebook every Sunday morning at 10 a.m. ET. At first, I thought of the series as a short-term way for visitors to feel as if they were here. Then, new viewers started tuning in from around the world, growing our family beyond my wildest dreams, and the show continues. It's so gratifying to see how the animals and their inspirational stories and antics bring people together of different backgrounds, cultures, and circumstances. We think of our interactive viewers as extended family, and thank them wholeheartedly for their interest, friendship, and support.

Thank you to my dear friend Marjorie Preston for sharing your passion, talents, and creativity in bringing this story to the world.

Above all, I thank my mother, Anne McNulty. Mom set an example of courage and joy in living that continues to uplift me. Best of all, she set in motion a chain of compassion that continues to save lives. Thanks, Mom, for this wonderful, chaotic, unexpected life!